INKSTANDS
&
INKWELLS
A
COLLECTOR'S
GUIDE

INKSTANDS
&
INKWELLS
❧ A ❧
COLLECTOR'S
GUIDE

BY BETTY AND TED RIVERA

Crown Publishers, Inc. New York

To our sister *Catherine* and our cousin *Eleanor A. Burns,*
who led us to the first inkwell of our collection;
and to the memory of our parents,
Charles Henry and *Mary Burns Rivera*

© 1973 by Betty and Ted Rivera

Library of Congress Catalog Card Number: 72–96655
ISBN: 0–517–504197

Designed by Shari de Miskey

Published simultaneously in Canada by
General Publishing Company Limited

Printed in the United States of America

Acknowledgments

We wish to acknowledge the assistance, courtesy, and guidance extended us during the writing of this book by Virginia Wright and Carol Hull of the Corning Glass Museum; Isabel Shattuck, Museum of Fine Arts, Boston; David T. Owsley, Carnegie Institute Museum of Art; Jessie McNab, Metropolitan Museum of Art, New York City; James A. Bear, Thomas Jefferson Memorial Foundation; Karol A. Schmiegel, Winterthur; E. P. Hogan, International Silver Company; Anne M. Serio, Smithsonian Institution; John McKey II, The Carter's Ink Company; the staff at Colonial Williamsburg; United States Department of the Interior; and United States Department of the Treasury.

We also wish to thank our friend Robert Duplease, Torrington, Connecticut, for generously lending us inkstands from his personal collection to photograph for this book; Larry Lawrence, Southington, Connecticut, for his assistance in securing needed documentation; and Violet and Seymour Altman for allowing us to use a photograph from their book, *The Book of Buffalo Pottery.*

Our appreciation is also extended to photographers Thomas Budney and Gerald Rubens of Torrington, Connecticut, who worked diligently to meet the challenges of picturing so many difficult inkstands and wells, and to Eileen Mo, also of Torrington, for her fine drawings.

Among others to whom we are indebted are Esther Doyle Carey of the Torrington Library Staff; Catherine Calhoun, Curator of the Torrington Historical Society; John Houghmaster, North Troy, New York, and J. Fenton Williams, Torrington, Connecticut.

Finally, we owe much to our sister Catherine, whose assistance in our research and in typing the manuscript did so much to make this book possible.

Contents

Introduction

*L*ord Byron poetically pointed out the importance of ink: "One drop of ink makes thousands, perhaps millions, think." Words like these bring to mind such writers as Harriet Beecher Stowe penning her *Uncle Tom's Cabin;* Winston Churchill recording his thoughts for future stirring messages to England's House of Commons; or Beethoven setting down the notes of his *Emperor* Concerto—all works with far-reaching effect upon mankind.

The receptacles that, through the ages, have held this important liquid are of particular fascination. Many have significant historical associations with various cultures and peoples. Many reveal man's creative ingenuity, for he made them from countless different materials in both functional and decorative form, and they graphically reflect his progress through the ages. Today, these ink containers of old have become not only popular collectibles but decorative accessories of unusual interest and beauty.

Although we know that man, from as early as 1200 B.C., used "inks" of various kinds (mainly vegetable and fish dyes) in these receptacles, the origin of ink has never been incontrovertibly established. Thaddeus Davids, in his book *The History of Ink,* contends that "ink is history."

To inkwell collectors, the lack of documentation about the origin of ink appears to parallel the paucity of available information about ink containers. It is extremely difficult to obtain practical guidance about selecting them. Many books on antiques make scant mention of such containers; those that do give more detailed information about them usually deal with a particular type—frequently wells of great value in private collections—and so the poor collector has to locate and study many books to accumulate even a modest amount of reliable information. We hope this book will be a genuine help to inkwell collectors. It has been our aim to provide substantial information about wells of many types, their development, and their historical background.

Our main concern, however, has been to provide the inkwell collector with realistic data about the inkwells available to him in today's market at less than prohibitive prices; to assist him in identifying and evaluating them, and, in doing so, to make collecting inkwells the happy and profitable pastime that we know it can be.

1

Collecting Inkwells for
Pleasure and Profit

ur decision to collect inkwells was the result of our being captivated by the prismed elegance of sunlight streaming through a crystal well topped with a glinting silver lid.

This "captivation" occurred on an early autumn day, when the Connecticut countryside basked in a warm amber haze, at a topflight flea market in a Salisbury meadowland. Here, among pressed glass compotes, copper teapots, curly maple stands, Sheraton sideboards, and thousands of other antique items, we bought our first inkwell and unknowingly began a collection that now numbers about 350, a collection that has enriched our lives and filled us with the desire to know more and more about this fascinating subject. We have found wells made in so many sizes and shapes and of so broad a variety of materials that searching for still different ones is like a treasure hunt.

In the beginning, we expected to buy only crystal and silver wells, but as we looked at those made of English pottery, faience, bronze, silver, gold, and even papier-mâché, we could not resist their charm. Soon we were collecting wells of any type that were not prohibitively priced and that appealed to us aesthetically. We bought some wells about which we knew little because we instinctively felt they were good ones, and fortunately these proved to be excellent choices—far more valuable than we had believed them to be.

It is important for collectors to buy only wells that appeal to them historically, artistically, or for some other good reason, and not to be influenced by a dealer's "hard sell." If consideration is given to beauty, craftsmanship, quality, and aesthetic appeal, only "treasures" will be gathered. An inkwell or inkstand that is a monstrosity of design may have a place in a collection to represent a type, but one that is chosen because it is liked or to complement a desk is the wiser choice.

In selecting inkstands and wells, it is advisable to buy from dealers who mark their merchandise with price tags. Even when these objects are clearly marked with a price, however, the buyer has the privilege of inquiring about a discount. Many dealers these days give a discount when they learn that the buyer is a serious collector who may become a regular customer.

The prices of stands and wells have been much affected lately by the fact that dealers, unable to obtain good antiques otherwise, are buying articles from one another, particularly before the official opening hour of antique shows. The dealer who acquires items in this way adds a few dollars to their purchase price, which has usually been at discount—a practice common between dealers. After a stand or well has changed hands in this manner a number of times, its price naturally has soared. Dealers and serious collectors seem not to worry about this point, however, for in the years to come the scarcity of old inkwells and inkstands, as well as of other antique items, will ensure a satisfactory return on such investments.

The importance of selecting only quality inkstands and wells cannot be overemphasized—they are always the most successful investments. And if a collector intends to sell his collection at a later date and regards it largely as an investment, he will be far more likely to sell it readily if he has chosen only quality items.

One of our loveliest colored glass wells was selected in this way. Exquisitely designed, with French ormolu encasing its emerald green glass container, it is a seldom-found type of work (Illustration No. 96). When we bought it, we had no idea that its gilt "cage" was French ormolu or that, in ensuing years of collecting, we would not see another like it. Today, because it is a quality item and has aesthetic appeal, this green inkwell is worth at least three times what we paid for it. But inkwells in general are increasing in price even more rapidly than many other antiques, as the number of people collecting them during the past few years has substantially increased and the demand has become greater.

When considering the purchase of any inkwell or stand, make sure not only that its components are all present, but that they are the original ones and are in reasonably good condition. Buying "signed" pieces, such as those marked by L. C. Tiffany, is also a wise practice, for marks and/or signatures are proof that a stand was made by a certain firm or specific artisan. Such pieces are becoming scarcer as collectors become more knowledgeable.

The monetary worth of an antique, however, need not always be the main criterion for buying it. Many items do not have great financial value but are of considerable sentimental or historical interest. For example, the little traveling inkwells are not usually high in price, but they are nostalgic reminders of a mode of living of a time long past. Buying an antique purely to enjoy it can, of course, be the greatest investment of all.

The area in which an antique is bought often affects the price asked for it. Inkwells that were made by the Pairpoint Manufacturing Company in New Bedford, Massachusetts, are more available in that area than in Topeka, Kansas, and may sell for less there, since quantities of Pairpoint wells were supplied to New Englanders and now quite often emerge from New England attics. In short, the price of antiques depends largely on supply and demand.

New collectors are sometimes confused as to just what constitutes an antique. Dealers who sell only the highest-priced period pieces regard the cutoff date as 1830, the time when handcrafted articles began to give way to mechanically produced objects. By United States law, however, an antique is any article more than one hundred years old; import duty is not charged on antiques accompanied by verification that they fall into that age class. Recently, in common usage, the term "antique" has become more encompassing, including articles from late in the Victorian period. But such items more correctly classify as "collectibles" or, as they are sometimes called, "new antiques." In the case of inkstands and inkwells, many can be classified as true antiques; others made from about 1872 up to the advent of the fountain and ball-point pens, which made them obsolete, are "collectibles." Items imported from other countries after the year 1891 bear the name of the country of origin, in accordance with the McKinley Tariff Act.

Sharing with others the pleasures of collecting inkwells has, for us, proved one of the finest rewards of this pastime. Our friends delight in seeing each new well we buy. Some are interested enough to tell us about wells they come upon that they feel we might want. Several credit our collection with having stimulated their own interest in antiques.

Among the antique dealers whom we have met in our search for inkwell treasures, we have made a number of friends who have become interested in our collection. They call us "the inkwell people," and some of them kindly save wells for us that they believe will enhance our collection. Listening to their reminiscences about fine inkwell collections they have seen and about changes in prices over the years and the rise and fall of collecting fads has been a liberal education for us. We are also indebted to them for tips on identifying the various materials of which wells are made and for teaching us points to check.

One of the best places to meet dealers is at an antique show. These shows have been held in the United States for about sixty-five years, the first one being in New York City following the success of a similar exhibition in London. The twice-a-year New York Armory show is a direct descendant of the first New York show. For collectors, a show not only provides an opportunity to ask dealers some of the questions that have been puzzling them; it also offers under one roof a vast assemblage of fine-quality items that can be minutely examined and compared. The alert and observant beginning collector can thus acquire much information about antiques in a short span of time.

The pleasure of looking for inkwells (collectors tend to call them inkwells even when referring to inkstands and standishes) is heightened, too, by the experiences one has when buying them. We recall one sunny summer day when Massachusetts pastureland was plumed with clover and we stopped to browse in a dealer-friend's shop in Ashley Falls. While there, we looked at an English inkstand of wood fitted with one large crystal well with a hinged crystal lid.

Unfortunately, the well was stuck in the stand in the wrong position, and so the lid opened at an odd angle. Our friend offered it to us at a reasonable price. We felt that it was an unusually decorative piece, and the price was low, so we bought it. On a cold blustery day about eight months later when we were going over our collection, we noticed that the crystal well in this stand was no longer stuck. The heat of our warm house had caused the wood (swollen by the cold dampness of an English home) to contract, and the stand was now restored to its original state!

The associations formed and the friends we have made while collecting inkwells have added what we consider a rich bonus to our hobby. There is also the excitement of comparing your own collection of inkwells with another collector's; of discovering an unusual well or an outstandingly beautiful one at an antique show and sharing your pleasure with the dealer, who is happy to find a buyer and tell you all he knows about the item; and of being privileged to view another person's antiques as a result of your common interest in relics of the past. One acquaintance invited us to her home and showed us the first and only hatchment we have ever seen. (A hatchment is a panel bearing a dead person's coat of arms, formerly carried in the funeral procession of a member of a prominent family.) The hatchment had belonged in her husband's family and was cherished as a family keepsake to be passed on to her young son, who, she said, had the distinction of being a descendant of the first white boy born in Connecticut. This small brush with history familiarized us with an old custom that was new to us.

Collecting inkwells has extended our knowledge of all antiques. In learning to identify wells we have had to read many books and visit hundreds of antique shows and shops as well as a dozen or more museums. Only by studying inkwells and inkstands at close range does one learn to recognize the superior work of master craftsmen and become familiar with the characteristics of the various types of glass, porcelain, and other materials used. Such concentrated study has given us also a keener appreciation of the ingenuity and diligence of those long-gone craftsmen who managed to produce these beautiful objects without benefit of laborsaving devices and modern techniques.

The age of an inkwell can often be established by its shape, and so it is doubly important to read books on antiques and visit museums in order to learn the styles and shapes of articles pro-

duced during specific periods of history—an inkwell usually con-
formed to the style popular at the time it was made. The Metropolitan Museum of Art in New York City and the Museum of Fine Arts
in Boston both have inkwells of various materials in their collections, as do many other museums around the country. For the study
of glass, the Carnegie Institute Museum of Art in Pittsburgh and
the Toledo Museum of Art in Toledo, Ohio, as well as Vermont's
two famous museums—the Bennington Museum in Bennington and
the Shelburne Museum in Shelburne—offer definitive collections.
Inkwell collectors should not fail to visit The Henry Francis du Pont
Winterthur Museum, Winterthur, Delaware, a depository of American decorative arts with numerous inkwell inclusions, and the justly
famed Henry Ford Museum in Dearborn, Michigan, with its fine
glass specimens.

In the past, little emphasis has been placed on visiting the
headquarters of small-town historical societies, but lately many of
these local groups have, with prideful enthusiasm, refurbished their
headquarters and given prominence to antique items of local manufacture or historical significance, including inkwells and ink bottles.
Often these headquarters have specimens of wares that are not seen
in larger museums, for these specimens are generally given to the
historical societies by local residents who want to preserve articles
that figured in local history and that they feel should be displayed
in their native locale.

Serious collectors often plan their vacations to include museum
visits. On one holiday trip, we visited the Sandwich Glass Museum
in Sandwich, Massachusetts, and, on another, the Corning Museum
at Corning, New York, where we could study specimens of glass
from earliest times to the present and learn from watching glass
being made. Even if a vacation is not specifically planned to include
museum visits, inkwell collectors can seldom resist seeking out any
antique shops in their vicinity. On a visit to Bermuda, we hired a
taxi so that we might cover the antique shops on this tiny archi-
pelago. In a shop in Hamilton, we found a rectangular traveling
inkwell of glass and silver of English origin, which is now one of our
choice vacation mementoes. Dealers in Bermuda told us that very
few Bermudian antiques are sold, for most of the people cherish
their family possessions and do not readily part with them—an
understandable attitude, since almost all the wares used there have
had to be imported.

Developing a sharp eye or a sixth sense for what will be avidly collected in the future can prove profitable even to the beginning collector on a small budget because tomorrow's high-priced "hot" items can generally be bought at bargain prices today. For one example, not too long ago Art Deco inkwells (of the 1930s period) could be bought very cheaply; anyone who had the foresight to invest in a few of them at that time could sell them at a tidy profit today, though they can still be bought now at lower prices than wells of greater age.

Such bargains should not be confused with the so-called "bargains" sometimes offered by certain dealers. Good antiques are rarely offered at bargain prices, and unless the collector is expert enough to know that the item offered at an unusually low price is genuine and sound and well worth that price, he should avoid buying it. Always keep in mind that most dealers of good reputation are knowledgeable about the articles they are selling. "Outsmarting" them is not easy, and collectors who feel they can acquire a bargain in this way run great risks. Veteran collectors know this and do not engage in such contests.

We have sometimes ordered inkwells by mail in response to advertisements in such reputable magazines as *Hobbies,* and thus obtained specimens we had been unable to locate at shops and shows. Only once or twice have we been disappointed in what we bought by mail. Some mail-order dealers have gone to the trouble of sending us photos and descriptions of wells that have come into their possession, with the thought that they might be suitable for our collection.

The realm of inkwells is an overlapping one. Interest in a Staffordshire well can quickly lead to a consuming desire for the Staffordshire villas that once graced the mantels of most English cottages. The acquisition of a silver-lidded well may turn one into an avid collector of the closely related silver-capped English scent bottles of cut glass. The history-minded collector may suddenly find himself also collecting factual tidbits about inks, such as that in pre-Christian times values and symbols were attached to the various colors—green ink denoted freshness, vigor and prosperity; blue, revelation; purple, royalty; and scarlet stood for blood and human life. Later, the Christians developed their own ink symbolism: fire and love were signified by red ink, life and hope by green, sorrow by violet, and death and destruction by black.

*   *   *

There is a vast difference between good and mediocre antique shows. Usually the admission price or the name of the show director is an adequate clue. As for flea markets, they have generally degenerated during the past few years, but there are still excellent ones in every section of the country, much like our favorite, which is held annually in a cow pasture in Salisbury, Connecticut. For us, that yearly market is the reliving of a memorable occasion, the purchase of our first inkwell. It is, as well, a reminder of our many other happy experiences as inkwell collectors.

2

Silver and Gold Inkstands
and Inkwells

During the eighteenth century British royalty customarily turned to glinting gold and silver inkstands as suitable gifts and presentation pieces, for such stands possessed a truly regal magnificence. For the signing of our own Declaration of Independence in 1776 a sterling silver inkstand of elegant simplicity was used; it had been designed in 1752 by Philip Syng, Jr., one of the most famous eighteenth-century American silversmiths, for the Pennsylvania Assembly. Early in the 1800s, after the signing of the various treaties of the Congress of Vienna, an inkstand was made from the metal of twenty-two diamond-studded portrait snuffboxes and presented, in typical fashion, to statesman Viscount Castlereagh of England (Robert Stewart, a leader in organizing resistance against Napoleon) by the "Sovereigns whose arms are engraved hereon" as a memento of the historic occasion. For today's collectors such rare and historically significant inkstands are practically unattainable—being either the property of

1.   Inkstand made by Philip Syng, Jr., in 1752 by order of the Assembly of Pennsylvania. It was used by the signers of the Declaration of Independence and the Constitution. *Independence National Historical Park Collection, Philadelphia*

museums or securely held in outstanding private collections. But there are still, fortunately, fine old silver and gold inkstands to be found.

Previous to the sixteenth century, it was considered undignified for an aristocrat to do his own writing. Scriveners fulfilled the duties of correspondents, and thus the inkstand—or standish, as it was called—was not in great demand as an ornament. By the end of the sixteenth century in England, the silver inkstands were made in the shape of a box, which contained an inkpot, wafer box (to hold paste wafers for sealing letters), and a sander (for powdered gum sandarac was used to keep the ink from spreading on uncalendered —unglazed—paper). The box was also fitted with a drawer for quills and sealing wax.

Few inkstands made by English silversmiths prior to the seventeenth century survive today. One of the earliest still extant was made by William Rainbow in 1630. In his book *The History of English Plate* (volume 2), Sir Charles James Jackson, F. S. A., says this stand is "the earliest silver inkstand known to the author." Properly designated as a Charles the First inkstand, it has a leaf-shaped base with cylindrical ink and sand vessels, plus a double bow engraved with the arms of Tracy. In the center are two cylinders forming penholders connected by a ring with a small figure or cupid in the center and plaques pierced with hearts and trefoils below. For a time in 1929 this inkwell was exhibited at Seaford House and Lansdown House, where it was the property of Michael Noble (formerly it was part of the celebrated collection of the late Sir John Noble).

Inkstands resembling casters with cruets were also made during the seventeenth century. Silversmith John Coney of Boston

2. Silver inkstand by W. R., London, 1630. This is considered the oldest date known for a surviving English silver inkstand. *Courtesy, Museum of Fine Arts, Boston*

made a stand of similar styling during the eighteenth century. A well-known example of what is called the "cruet-type" inkstand has three cylindrical vessels—one for ink, another with perforated top for use as a sand-caster, and the third, it is believed, for wafers.

Plain little inkstands dating to the early part of the seventeenth century are mentioned in old records as "miscellaneous plate [solid silver] around the house." They were choice items of display in the homes of the wealthy of that period.

Inkstands developed rapidly during the eighteenth century, and came into their own. During these years appeared the casket-type inkstand with its fitted enclosed inkpot, sand-caster, and wafer box. Sometimes it had a slide-out drawer to hold sealing wax. The deep-dished tray-type inkstand with bullet feet in varying shapes and sizes was also used.

A bell was another eighteenth-century addition to an inkstand, a typical Georgian touch of elegance. It was used to summon a servant when a letter was ready for posting. The Georgian years also brought a shallow tray-type inkstand, which had bowed (canoe-shaped) ends and reeded rims, reflecting the neoclassic design popular at that time. In the 1740s, rococo designs initiated the use of a tray with scrolled or knurled feet and reeded rims. A dished channel running along the front or the rear of the tray (at times, along both) was developed as a convenient place to keep the pen-knife needed to sharpen a blunted quill. Some inkwell and inkstand collectors enjoy acquiring penknives to supplement their collection, and it is interesting to learn in Therle Hughes's *Small Decorative Antiques* that the penknives of the Georgian period sometimes had not only an ivory handle but also an ivory sheath to protect the blade.

One of the largest inkstands ever made was executed during the eighteenth century by Paul de Lamerie, a French Huguenot who emigrated to England. Commissioned by members of the nobility to create elaborate and highly decorative silver pieces, he was considered the "leading spirit of rococo," but not all his work was in that style—he also produced many charming functional articles of simple beauty. Today his work is more avidly sought than that of any other English silversmith. Although many authorities feel that it is not the most superior work, amazingly high prices are paid for his silver creations.

During the eighteenth century in America, the word "standish"

3.   Silver standish (1733–34) by Paul de Lamerie consists of a silver tray holding a pouncepot, an inkpot, and a bell. *The Smithsonian Institution*

4.   Georgian sterling silver inkstand, 10 inches long. The two crystal wells have hinged silver lids. The bases of the wells, silver capped, fit into silver holders that are part of the canoe-shaped stand.

5.   George II silver standish with taperstick and two pots, made by John Jacobs, London, 1748, which bears the arms of Mary Anglesy Uxbridge. It is 13 inches long and 9¾ inches wide. *Carnegie Institute Museum of Art, Ailsa Mellon Bruce Collection*

6.   Eighteenth-century silver inkstand with two open-capped pressed glass wells and a silver wafer box with hinged lid of silver. Stand is 9¾ inches long, and almost 4 inches wide. The wafer box and well holders are fastened in place by a silver rod on the underside of the stand that runs through slots in the base of each well holder and in the feet of the wafer box. No identifying mark.

was replaced by the word "inkstand." An advertisement by Williamsburg printers in 1764 offered a "large Silver fashioned Ink Stand" at one pound ten shillings. American silversmiths, however, gave small attention to making inkwells during the early years of the Republic. Silver was scarce and was used for more "sensible" household items. It was only natural, though, as the years passed, for eighteenth-century men of letters who raised their own and America's standard of living during that day to want prestigious writing accouterments. And when cabinetry in the style of such skilled craftsmen as Chippendale, Hepplewhite, and Sheraton began to fill American mansions, inkstands of various types—including those of silver and crystal—became fitting accessories. Cut glass pots with silver mounts, which were an innovation of the eighteenth century, glinted in their shining silver stands on writing tables or desks and lent distinction to the library or office of an American landowner, merchant, or statesman.

In the nineteenth century, many inkstands were made as large circular trays with scalloped rims and chased designs. Often there was a platform in the center of the tray that supported two inkpots and two quill holders. A smaller central pedestal might hold a taperstick for convenient usage.

The steel pen was introduced in this country about 1809, but the inkstand with sander and quill remained in use as late as the third decade of the nineteenth century. When the fountain pen arrived, the inkstand had little practical purpose, and of course the advent of the ball-point pen relegated the stand to the realm of the decorator and collector.

Silvermaking was revolutionized in 1742 by the development of Sheffield plate, a fusion of copper and silver. Quite accidentally in that year (as the story goes), an English cutler, Thomas Boulsover, while repairing a silver and copper knife handle, overheated it and found that the two metals adhered. When he was unsuccessful in separating them, he decided to capitalize on this metal affinity, and commenced by manufacturing buttons, which are regarded today as the earliest examples of Sheffield plate. The word "plate" had previously applied to solid silver; technically, it is also correct for Sheffield, for the dictionary defines plate as "a flat or nearly flat and relatively thin piece of material, originally only of metal."

The production of Sheffield plate was fostered by the city of Sheffield, but the plate was also produced in other places in En-

7. Fine English sterling silver inkstand approximately 11 inches long including the handles. The two 2¼-inch wells have substantial silver-beaded collars and hinged lids. Circa 1857. T. J. Barnard hallmarks on stand and inkwells.

8. Sheffield silver box-type inkstand, more than 5½ inches long, includes two crystal wells. Unmarked.

9. Heavily embossed Sheffield silver inkstand, about 10½ inches long and 6 inches wide. The tall etched glass well with loose cover is 2½ inches high. Marked "Elkington & Co."

gland. Among its advantages were cheap production costs—it contained a considerable amount of copper in its base and, unlike solid silver, it was not taxable. As might be expected, therefore, people of lower income could buy it, though previously silver had been within the reach of only wealthy people.

About 85 percent of Sheffield plate is unmarked; the remaining 15 percent sometimes bears the name of the maker and sometimes has pseudo-hallmarks that are deliberately indistinguishable or misleading. Today's collector must be cautious when buying Sheffield plate. This fused ware must not be confused with copper that has been plated with silver or with silverplate misleadingly called "Real Sheffield," "Sheffield," or "Genuine Sheffield Plate." Always keep in mind that Sheffield plate was produced for somewhat less than one hundred years, and, because of its fragility during the early years of production, few pieces made during that period have survived. The technique of making Sheffield plate, however, has not been lost. It is still used in rare instances, probably by descendants of those who once earned their living by making it.

Inkstands of Sheffield plate were at first flimsy and poorly produced, so it is small wonder that few now exist. In style they resemble the solid silver inkstands with pierced decoration (most Sheffield plate followed the silver styles in existence from 1740 to 1838). During the 1800s, the process of Sheffield plating was improved. The inkstands made then consisted of an under tray, which contained two wells and a taper box. Some also had wafer boxes surmounted by a taperstick. Stands made during the early part of the eighteenth century were small; larger ones emerged in the later years of the Sheffield production, including the "ambassador" type—an impressive stand with much elaborate decoration and a removable drawer. Most inkstands of this plate were oblong, but about three years ago we discovered a fine example of a boat-shaped Sheffield plate inkstand made about 1780. Globular inkstands (the globelike well is enclosed between circular folding sides and mounted on a foot) are a type of Sheffield inkstand rarely seen outside a fine private collection or a museum.

Sheffield "frauds" are not as common as might be expected. Silver connoisseurs know that old pieces of Sheffield have a bluish tint whereas electroplate is much whiter in color. Electroplate is also heavier than Sheffield, and Sheffield is heavier than solid silver. The carefully joined seams apparent in both Sheffield and old silver are not discernible in electroplate, on which the silver surface covering the entire item is unbroken. The thin rim of silver that is folded along the edges of an article to conceal the copper base is not always a foolproof means of identifying Sheffield plate. Early pieces do not have it; and anyone interested in faking Sheffield would not find this rim difficult to duplicate.

The process of Sheffield plating was virtually discarded when, about 1840, the English firm of Elkington and Company began making silverplate by electrolysis. It had been discovered that with silver as the positive pole, a galvanic current sent through a bath of potassium cyanide would deposit silver on the article to be plated, which could be copper but was usually white metal or britannia. Electroplate was cheaper to make than Sheffield plate—articles could be sold for a fifth or a sixth of the price of solid silver pieces.

Unlike Sheffield plate, the new electroplate did not follow the traditional styles but appeared in many new and different designs. Prior to the last quarter of the nineteenth century, its quality approached perfection, but as the demand grew, many makers sacrificed good styling and went in for the overornamentation that characterized the last years of the Victorian era.

American electroplate is superior to English electroplate. Production was begun in this country by Reed and Barton, Meriden Britannia, and Rogers Brothers soon after the process was introduced in England. Such well-known companies as Oneida, Gorham, and Rice became important makers of electroplate in the post–Civil War years. Gorham produced the highest grade (although production continued for only a few years) and, like Reed and Barton, used a heavy nickel base—at that time, the base metal determined the value of a piece.

Reed and Barton and Middletown Silver Plate Company exhibited ornate pieces of electroplate at the Philadelphia Centennial Exhibition in 1876. This "started the ball rolling" as far as American housewives were concerned. Soon every family that could afford it

►

10, 11. Pages from the 1877 catalog of the Meriden Britannia Company, Meriden, Conn. This company was founded in 1852, but did not advertise inkstands until 1877. *International Silver Company, Meriden, Connecticut*

No. 1. LIBRARY SET, COMPLETE.

CANDLE STICK.	INK STAND.	CANDLE STICK.
el Finish, each, . . $6.75	Steel Finish, each, . . $6.75	Steel Finish, each, . . $6.75

ELECTRO SILVER PLATE.

No. 25.	No 24.
ountain Ink, ... $4.75	Fountain Ink, ... $4.25

had an electroplated tea set, an impressive centerpiece, or a revolving caster to lend an elegant touch to the table. The glass containers for these casters and the glass wells for inkstands were made by American manufacturers.

Electroplated inkstands are available today for collecting, but there are not as many as might be expected. These stands were not found in every home during the Victorian era, but were usually the cherished possessions of the upper middle class and people of considerable means. Often they were used for presentation pieces to mark a special occasion, as awards to encourage business, or as trophies for sporting events. Presentation pieces frequently have historic interest and so are prized by history-oriented collectors. If one can afford them, silver inkstands are preferable to collect because of the currently high value of silver, but silverplated inkstands also merit attention.

Many old inkstands are imported from England today, among them electroplated specimens that sometimes have silver or glass fittings. These are important-looking pieces and well worth the prices asked for them. Generally they have been resilvered and are in excellent condition.

The type of decoration on an electroplated inkstand is sometimes indicative of the years when it could have been made. In the 1860s, surface designs were chased or cut; borders were foliated, beaded, or gadrooned. In the 1870s figures of animals, men, and exotic birds were mounted on inkstands and other items, and surface motifs included ferns, flowers, and grasses in bright-cut designs on a "frosted" background. Later, repoussé (embossed) and hammered designs were introduced, along with heavy grape motifs for borders. Although some of these stands may appear ostentatious in styling and overly large, others have a graceful beauty and superior quality; some are so unusual in design as to merit a place in any collection.

The acquisition of silver inkstands, whether plated, Sheffield, or solid silver, requires at least a rudimentary knowledge of silver

►

12.   Page from the 1877 catalog of the Meriden Britannia Company. *International Silver Company, Meriden, Connecticut*

INKSTANDS.

No. 4.

Silver, ... $3.50

No. 14.

Silver, ... $4.50

Gold and Steel Finish, . . 6.00

No. 1. Gold and Steel Finish, . . $6.00

No. 3. Gold and Steel Finish, small size, 4.50

No. 22.

Silver, ... $8.50

Gilt, ... 9.50

Gold and Steel Finish, . . 10.00

No. 26.

Silver, ... $8.50

Gold and Steel Finish, . . 10.00

No. 21.

Silver, ... $9.00

Gilt, ... 10.00

Gold and Steel Finish, . . 10.50

No. 20.

Gilt, ... $8.00

No. 18.

Silver, ... $9.00

Gilt, ... 10.00

Gold and Steel Finish, . . 10.50

No. 19.

Silver, ... $9.00

Gilt, ... 10.00

GOLD AND SILVER PLATE.

(ONE-THIRD SIZE.)

No. 41.
Hammered, . . $5.50 (ANCKISS).
Hammered, Gold Inlaid, 6.50 (ASPEN).

No. 29.
Gold and Silver, $3.50 (PITCH).

No. 30.
Gold and Silver, $4.50 (PISTOL).

No. 40.
Silver, $4.50 (ASTUTE).
Gold Inlaid, 5.00 (ATHLETE).

No. 45.
Old Copper and Gold, $8.50 (CAPOTE).
Old Silver and Gold, 9.00 (CAPABLE).

No. 32.
Silver, . . $8.00 (PLASTER).
Gilt, . . 9.00 (PLASTIC).

No. 38. OLD SILVER.
Hammered, . . $9.00 (ASSUME).
Hammered, Gold Inlaid, 10.50 (ASTONISH).

No. 39.
Silver, . . $8.00 (ASPHALT).
Gold Lined, . 9.00 (ASSEMBLY).

No. 46. WITH LETTER SCALE.
Hammered, Old Copper and Gold, $9.50 (CAPACITY).
Hammered, Old Silver and Gold, 10.00 (CALIPERS).

No. 42. WITH LETTER SCALE.
Silver, . . $10.00 (PETITION).
Old Silver, . 11.00 (PETREL).

No. 48.
Enameled Copper, Old Silver Mountings, $7.50 (CAPRICE).

No. 28.
Silver, . . $9.00 (PLANET).
Gold and Steel, . 10.50 (PLANK).

No. 51.
Old Silver, . . $18.00 (CASTE).
Gold Inlaid, . . 20.00 (CHOICELY).
(One-Third Size.)

No. 18.
Old Silver, . . $9.00 (FLACID).
Gold Inlaid, . . 10.00 (PLAIT).

(202)

13. Silver plate and gold inkstands from the 1877 catalog of the Meriden Britannia Company. *International Silver Company, Meriden, Connecticut*

INK STANDS.

(HALF SIZE).

TRADE MARK
WHITE METAL

TRADE MARK
NICKEL SILVER.

No. 43.
Old Copper, . . $3.50 (CASEMATE)
Old Silver, . . 4.00 (CASEMENT)

No. 31.
Silver, Gold Inlaid, $6.25 (FISTON).

No. 44.
Old Copper, . . $4.50 (CASTAWAY).
Old Silver, . . 5.00 (CASTIGATE).

No. 47.
Enameled Copper, Old Silver Mountings, $4.75 (CHEST)

No. 49.
Old Silver, . . $8.50 (CASSIMERE).
Gold Inlaid, . . 10.00 (CASSINO).

No. 37.
Old Silver, . . $6.00 (PLATONIC)

	PAGE, ETC.
ICE BOWLS, ...	16–245
ICE CREAM DISHES, .	49, 50, and 189, 190
ICE CREAM KNIVES, .	. (SEE) Flat Ware.
ICE PITCHERS, . . .	" Pitchers.
ICE PITCHER SETS, .	. " Pitchers.
ICE TILTING SETS, .	. " Pitchers.
ICE TUBS, ...	16
ICE URNS, . . .	(SEE) Pitchers.
INDIVIDUAL BUTTER DISHES, .	47–48
INDIVIDUAL BUTTER PLATES, .	47–48
INDIVIDUAL SUGARS, . .	200
INDIVIDUAL CASTERS, .	104–107
INK STANDS, ...	201–202

For Flat Ware see last pages of this Catalogue.

No. 36.
Old Silver, . . $5.50 (PLATINA).
Old Silver, Gold Inlaid, 6.50 (PLATING).

No. 50.
Old Silver, . . $10.50 (CASHBOOK).
(Half Size.)

No. 35.
Old Silver, . . $4.50 (PLAT).
Old Silver, Gold Inlaid, 5.50 (PLATE).

(201)

14.   Page of inkstands from the 1877 Meriden Britannia Company catalog.
International Silver Company, Meriden, Connecticut

hallmarks, especially if the stands are bought from dealers who themselves have scant knowledge of silver. Hallmarks are official symbols stamped on gold and silver articles attesting to their place of origin, maker, date, and purity. The system originated in England in 1335, when marks were applied at the Goldsmiths Company in London on articles sent there to be tested, to ascertain that the correct standards were being adhered to by the maker. The use of hallmarks was also intended to combat the sale of counterfeit articles and to show that certain legal obligations had been fulfilled. The system is a complex one but well worth study by anyone who collects English silver. A great many devices have been used since the marking system was begun, and for help in identifying these

15. Gracefully designed silver-plated English inkstand is 7 inches long, 1½ inches high, and 2 inches wide, including the claw feet. The stamp or wafer compote in the center is almost 3 inches in diameter. The ribbed glass wells (1¾ inches square) sit down a half-inch below the surface of the stand. Including their hinged lids, they are slightly over 2 inches in height. Unmarked; circa 1880.

16. Silver-plated casket-type inkstand accommodates two wells with Sheffield tops. Stand is 4¾ inches long, 2½ inches wide, and about 3¼ inches high, including the round knob on the cover. Marked "England."

marks we recommend *The Book of Old Silver* and *The Book of Sheffield Plate*, both by Seymour B. Wyler.

In America the early silversmith's mark was usually his initial or surname in relief on a depressed oval, heart, rectangle, or shield.

Collectors of silver and silverplated inkstands will find the following information of particular interest:

Silver plate is 1000 parts fine—that is, entirely silver. The metal was obtained by melting down Spanish coins, "plata," which were given in exchange for British cargoes in the West Indies and South America in centuries past. Silver plate fashioned into untensils is called "domestic plate."

Coin silver refers to silver having the same content as English coins—900 parts silver to 100 parts base metal. In America "coin," "pure coin," "dollar," or the initial "C" or "D" sometimes was stamped on silver after 1830. This meant that the ware was made from melted coin of the same quality as coin from the United States Mint, which was 900 fine or 900 parts pure silver out of 1000.

The word *sterling* is derived from the name of the old English penny. It was first stamped on silver in England in 1850 to show quality—925 parts silver to 75 parts alloy, which is the same content used in the United States for sterling silver. The word "sterling" did not come into use in the United States until 1860.

The novice should make sure that any inkwell offered as sterling is stamped "sterling." In this way, until he has acquired a working knowledge of hallmarks and a "feel" for silver, he will not be so likely to go astray.

Electroplated ware is usually marked. Prior to 1860, the marks were placed on disks soldered to the bottom of the piece, but after that date they were cut into the bottom of the piece. The mark included the maker's name and trademark. Frequently, it also included an indication of the type of plate—triple or quadruple (the depth of the plate changed the value of a piece). The base metal used in shown by letters—EPN (electroplate, nickel), EPC (copper), and EPWM (white metal).

In England "F" was sometimes marked on silver to denote that it was of foreign origin and might not meet English purity standards.

Silversmithing existed as far back as the fifth century in Europe, but very few examples of early Continental silver still remain. Wars and political and religious struggles for power plus dire economic conditions often resulted in the melting down of art treasures. Few records survived these centuries of turmoil, so it is difficult to discuss early Continental pieces. From time to time, European silver inkstands made in later years are seen at antique shows and shops. Recently we saw one made in Italy for a noble family, probably one of the largest and most magnificent silver stands we have ever seen. Oval in shape, it was about 15 inches long and styled somewhat like an Italian fountain. Though not commonly seen on the market, silver stands from any foreign country are worth adding to a general collection of inkstands, but are particularly appropriate for a collection of silver stands.

Visiting museums, antique shows, and antique shops will help the collector develop acumen in buying silver inkstands and wells. He will soon learn, for example, that many of the little crystal wells sold singly these days are actually wells separated from their stands. He will also learn which types of wells and stands are most frequently available and the prevailing price for them. Sometimes stands alone are offered for sale, but unless the collector welcomes a challenge he should not be tempted by them. Finding single wells of the proper size to complete a stand is growing increasingly difficult.

17.   Silver stand, 12¼ inches long and slightly more than 2 inches wide, holds two twelve-sided clear glass wells, which are 2¼ inches in height, including their silver tops. Hallmarked. In the foreground (*left to right*) are three clear crystal wells, all with silver lids, the first well being Baccarat in the famous Swirl pattern. Though this pattern is characteristically associated with Baccarat, not all Swirl-pattern glass is Baccarat. American pressed glass wells with separate lids of this design are also on the market today. The hexagonal inkwell in the center, 3¼ inches high, has a star cut in the base and an elaborately embossed hinged lid. The round well at the far right, with mushroom-shaped hinged lid and Harvard cut base, is 3 inches in diameter and 4 inches high.

18. An elaborate silver-plated English inkstand has two wells with hinged lids flanking a graceful reclining deer. Stand is 8¼ inches long by about 5 inches wide, and is signed "Philip Ashberry & Sons"; also marked "Sheffield" and trademarked "Britannia."

19. Sterling silver inkstand, more than 5½ inches long, 4¼ inches wide at the widest point, is bordered by a graceful gallery. The cut glass well is 2 inches by 1¾ inches. The silver lid is hinged. Hallmarked by Gorham with lion passant, anchor, and Gorham "G."

20. English silver-plated oval stand, 7½ inches long, 5¾ inches wide, has two 1½-inch-square wells, 1¾ inches high including the hinged silver covers. Each well is held in place by a ½-inch-high silver gallery. In the center is an attached taperstick. The stand bears the "F.BRS." hallmark, plus "S" (Sheffield) and "E.P." (Electroplate). 1890.

The sand-caster is often referred to as a pounce pot—pounce was powdered cuttlefish bone or powdered gum sandarac used to keep ink from spreading over the paper. At first the holes in pounce pots were round; by 1730, they had sawtooth edges; and by 1760 the holes were curved in shape. Among other tidbits of knowledge that the collector should know are these: A high-priced stand with crystal wells should have lids or stopper in keeping with the design of the entire stand; if the wells are not affixed to the stand, they should fit snugly; the age of a stand is not established merely by the presence of a taper holder, a wafer box, or some other "period" inclusion—these parts are included in both the old specimens and modern reproductions.

During the latter part of the Victorian era and the early years of the twentieth century, quantities of single wells of silver were made by numerous silver manufacturers. Although not as impressive looking as the elaborate silver inkstands of the same period, these single wells, sometimes of unusual or fanciful design, have an

21.   Silver-plated pad-foot stand, 8½ inches long and just over 6 inches wide, holds two crystal wells, 2 inches square and 2½ inches high. The mushroom-shaped hinged lids are silver. Stand is marked "Philip Ashberry & Sons/Sheffield," and bears a "Britannia" trademark.

22.   At left is a Gorham sterling silver and crystal inkwell with unusual alternating swirls of crystal and silver and an onion-shaped, hinged, swirled silver lid. In the center is a London silver inkwell (1846) with hallmark; makers, Charles T. Fox and George Fox. Ornately pierced sterling silver covers the cobalt blue glass well, which has a star-cut base. The heavy silver lid is hinged. Exquisitely worked, pierced disk under the lid fits over the well to form the top. Two quills can be accommodated by the holders attached to the two sides. The traveling inkwell (*right*) of sterling silver repoussé has a spring-released hinged lid. Marked "Theodore B. Starr."

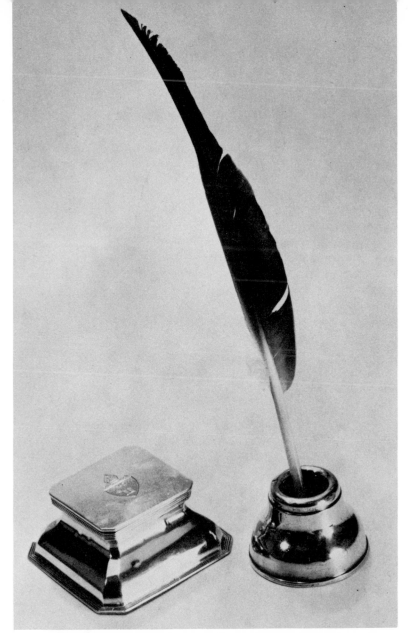

23. Four-inch-square sterling silver inkstand has a bishop's crest engraved on the hinged lid. The hallmark "J.G. & S." appears inside the cover, on the front of the stand, and on the underside. The round glass well (*right*) is covered with sterling silver hallmarked "T.H.H." The funnel-shaped mouth of the well is uncovered. Diameter at bottom, 2¾ inches.

understated beauty that makes them desirable additions to a collection. Many were presentation pieces like the older stands of silver, and they too are often inscribed with dates and messages. Our collection boasts a silver single well about 4 inches square at the base and tapering to a 2½-inch square lid engraved with a replica of a bishop's ecclesiastical seal (Illustration No. 23). It was probably given to a bishop by his parishioners to commemorate some anniversary, in recognition of his devoted service.

A new type of handcrafted silverware developed by The Gorham Manufacturing Company appeared on the market around 1901. Called Martele, this new ware had a silver content of 950–1000 (higher than sterling silver), and it was expensive. In design, it followed the handsome naturalistic lines of the then-popular Art Nouveau style, with flower and leaf-form decorations (including pond lilies, daises, and the like) and wave and cloud effects.

24. Victorian silver-plated inkstand, 6½ inches long, 5¼ inches wide, has two 1½-inch clear cut glass wells with hinged silver lids. Unmarked.

25. The crystal well at left, 2½ inches high, is partly covered with romantically embossed silver. The hinged silver lid is also embossed. Marked "Germany" and with an unidentified hallmark. The slightly smaller (2 inches square) crystal well at center fits into a 1½-inch-high silver-plated holder embossed with a design of windmills and flowers; the hinged lid is similarly embossed. At right, the paperweight-type inkwell (3½ inches in diameter) with a star design on the base has a wide sterling silver collar decorated with intricate floral and scroll motifs. The hinged silver lid bordered with scroll and floral openwork is monogrammed in the center.

26. Sterling silver embossed desk set includes tray and inkwell, blotter, and stamp box, the last three pieces monogrammed. The tray is 9½ inches long; the crystal well is about 3½ inches square and has a hinged silver lid.

It is known that Gorham made inkwells in this art silver line, but to date we have not seen any of them. If found today, they would be highly collectible, as collectors are becoming increasingly interested in Martele because of its silver content, fine construction, and beauty of design. All Art Nouveau silver is considered collectible today, but Martele is choice.

Martele was sold by jewelers, and many items—probably including inkwells—were made especially for Spaulding & Company of Chicago and Theodore B. Starr of New York (a company that sold many inkwells). Such articles are easily indentifiable, for each piece carries the specific company's name in addition to the usual Gorham lion, anchor, and G. A spread-winged eagle was also shown, over which the word Martele sometimes appears, and below which is the marking "950–1000 fine."

Stands of solid gold are beyond the realm of purchase for most

27. Gold-plated inkstand of restrained elegance.

collectors, but of late years the English have gold-plated some of the old stands from the Victorian period, and these make particularly handsome specimens. Several years ago, we bought an old brass stand that is gold-plated. It is about fourteen by eight inches in size, and has double melon-shaped wells on a footed, decorated tray. (See Color Plate 7.)

Our collection includes another gold-plated brass stand that is oval in shape, and measures nine inches long and four inches wide, circa 1895. Four golden tassels form the feet of this stand, which is edged in a solid unbroken chain, as is the urn-shaped well. The hinged cover is round with a disklike finial. The gold-plating lifts these stands above the commonplace.

Generally, the finest stands and wells are to be found in the most elegant and high-priced antique shops. Do not be reluctant to visit such shops, even if you cannot afford the finest specimens at present. Most shopowners can recognize a serious collector and will realize that he is a potential future customer. Some, responding to an obviously genuine interest, will invite the visitor to view rare specimens not openly displayed. In any case, it costs nothing to look—and you may well learn a great deal.

28.   Three hard-to-find Victorian gilt inkstands (*left to right*): gilt combined with alabaster; gilt combined with crystal and an emeraldlike jewel; gilt combined with crystal and enamel.

3

Traveling Inkwells

hen Lincoln traveled to Gettysburg to deliver his famous address, his aide undoubtedly checked twice to be sure that the President had his inkwell with him. Until the fountain pen was popularly introduced in 1884 by L. E. Waterman of New York, traveling with one's own ink supply for writing with a sharpened quill, or a quill with a metal nib, was a necessity for the literate. There were diaries to keep up to date, eagerly awaited letters to write, and important documents to "sign and seal."

There is little documentation to indicate that travelers' wells came into use until the seventeenth century. The well emerged then as a part of a "box," sometimes called a "desque" or "cabinet," frequently made of silver, which was carried by travelers who prized their comfort and took along not only writing paper, quill pens, and ink but "medicaments," sewing necessities, and toiletries. And, as it was frequently cold in the inns and homes of those days,

29, 30, & 31. Thomas Jefferson's traveling desk with inkwell. *The Thomas Jefferson Memorial Foundation*

the traveler often made use of his writing box while he warmed himself before the fireplace during the evening.

In the eighteenth century, these boxes became known as compendiums. They were of more ornate design, covered with everything from embroidered cloth to veneers of tortoiseshell and ivory; some were even lavishly lined with lace. As the standard of living rose, they became highly decorated and sumptuously lined "carriage boxes" in which ladies could carry, in addition to their sewing materials, paper, ink, quills, medicines, and mirror, just about anything that would make a trip more comfortable. However, a humbler traveler would undoubtedly carry a small, plain well that adequately served its purpose.

Eighteenth-century daybook records kept by Williamsburg, Virginia, printers of those years reveal that in 1751 inkhorns were advertised for sale for a few shillings. The term "inkhorn" was used loosely to define either an ink container to be carried on the person or a small ink container for the table or desk, according to various eighteenth-century authorities, including Samuel Johnson and N. Bailey in his *Dictionarium Britannicum* (1730, London). During the sixteenth century, scriveners, in performing their writing duties for the nobility and wealthy (they were probably the first "public stenographers"), used inkhorns made of horn, which they found light in weight and practical for their purpose. But, by the eighteenth century, inkhorns were made of stone and glass as well as horn. Williamsburg printers' daybooks also reveal that the "best Edinburgh Inkpots, for the Pocket" were advertised for sale in 1775 for a few shillings. The material of which they were made is unfortunately not mentioned in these books.

After the Colonial period, when roads and modes of travel had improved, more and more people of lesser means began to take journeys. The tiny inkwell that could be safely tucked away in a carpetbag, valise, or pocket became a popular item. These little pocket wells, as they are sometimes called, vary in size, but usually are about two or three inches in width or diameter and just about as high. Securely fastened with ingeniously devised catches and locks, they were evidently made in flock quantity during the years that American settlements mushroomed into cities, sailing vessels bowed to steamers, and trains tooted their arrivals and departures to long lines of passengers at railroad depots. Such traveling wells

32.   Traveling inkwell, London, England (1814–15). On the bottom is inscribed "from the Gadshill Sale 1870"; on the side, "Charles Dickens." *The Metropolitan Museum of Art, Gift of Mrs. John C. Gray, 1910*

were made of everything from wood with glass or metal "inserts" (wells), to the gutta-percha that is especially collectible today. This was a whitish-to-brown substance resembling rubber that resisted corrosion by ink. During Victorian days, it was also popularly used to frame daguerreotypes. Gutta-percha wells were either round or oval in shape, varying in size from about one to two inches across and about equal in height to the width of the well. They had screw caps.

Many traveling wells were produced by S. Silliman & Company of Chester, Connecticut. The well-known barrel-shaped ones of rosewood, boxwood, or cocoawood are about two inches in height and have what a Silliman advertisement of the mid-1800s referred to as "screw tops" or "bayonet catches." The tiny bottles inside are released by a spring in the bottom of the container. Collecting these "lesser" traveling inkwells is a much easier and far less expensive hobby than acquiring rare eighteenth-century "desques." For the average modern collector, early boxes of fine craftsmanship are not only prohibitive in price; it is also difficult to store a sizable collection of them in a contemporary home.

Since the Middle Ages, leather has been a favorite covering for containers, and so it was only natural that it eventually came to be used to cover traveling wells of miniature size, fitted with snug inserts of various materials and often with spring or push-button locks. Although leather traveling wells are not as abundant as they used to be in antique shows and shops, they are still obtainable at modest prices. Some that are of tooled leather are in mint condition; others may be somewhat shabby from use, but a bit of wear should not materially affect their value. From our point of view, if wear is

33. Group of traveling inkwells: wooden, metal, leather-covered (including Florentine tooled), sterling silver, and brass. (See descriptions in text.)

34.   In the center is Worden's ink bottle with screw cap, and at left are
the two parts of the metal case into which it fits. Case is marked
"Worden's Bottle Case PAT'D July 28th, 1885." The case is 3 inches in
height. Pressed glass bottle at right with wood and cork stopper has a
nickel-plated case marked "Solid Drawn Metal Pat. June 20, 1882."

not excessive it is not objectionable—an old item that was often
used is bound to show some sign of wear. Before buying a traveling
well, however, always test the locking device thoroughly (if there is
one), and make sure the insert is present and in good condition.
Such factors do affect the value.

The Austrians and Germans made leather-covered traveling
wells that were sometimes "little works of art," with colorful mosaic
decoration on their white-metal lids. They have spring locks and,
like all such wells, glass inserts. One attractive well of this type has
the word "Carlsbad" spelled out in tan and red mosaic. It may well
be that these tiny wells were mostly souvenir pieces, as they were
easy to pack and bring home from a journey; probably many bore
the names of such famous sights as Trafalgar Square and Mont
Blanc, or of cities such as Paris or Vienna. We have not been able to
establish this point definitely, but it is a reasonable assumption.

The English also made leather-covered traveling wells that
were quality items, some even containing sanders of minute size.
Leather-covered novelty wells were made too. One was in the form
of a weight like those used to tether horses during the days when
the Main Streets of America were filled with horses and buggies

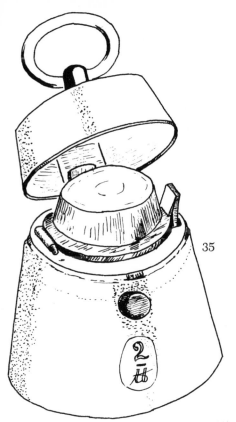

35

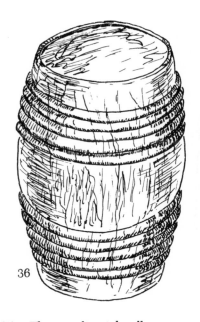

36

37

35, 36, & 37.   The traveling inkwell at upper left is covered with brown leather and has a brass ring on top of the hinged, spring-released lid. The traveling inkwell at right was made by S. Silliman & Co. This barrel-shaped well of rosewood is slightly over 2 inches high. The upper part of the barrel is the screw-on cap. The lower part holds a small glass bottle set atop a spring fastened in the bottom of the barrel. There is no lid or stopper for the bottle. When the cap (top of the barrel) is screwed onto the bottom, it presses the bottle securely against the spring and serves as a reliable seal. The novelty traveling well (*left*), about 4 inches in height, is designed to represent a bottle in a silver-plated wine cooler. It is marked with an anchor and fish. The upper part of the cooler and the bottle form the outside lid; both inner and outer lids are spring-hinged.

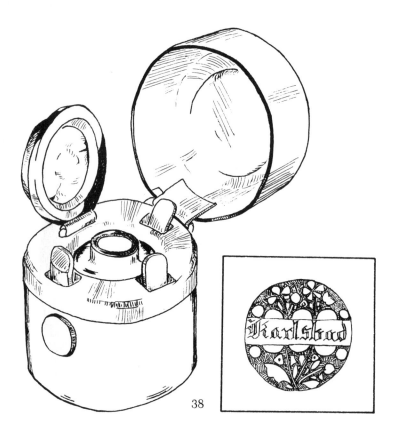

38

"tied up" outside stores and offices. Its leather is a ruddy red, and the brass hook on the top is a replica of the large one on a real horse weight to which a rope was attached.

During the War Between the States, soldiers carried small cylindrical wells generally made of wood with glass inserts, some of which were produced by S. Silliman & Company. The well, a penholder with a metal nib, and a supply of stationery were carried in the soldier's knapsack in the early days of the war when his uniform was trim and strictly "regulation." But as the war progressed and uniforms and equipment grew ragged—and the soldier himself increasingly footsore and weary—the knapsack was often abandoned. Very practically, he then put his inkwell, pen, and paper in the small roll he carried with his other possessions, and traveled "light." In a room at the Bennington (Vermont) Museum filled with oddments of Americana (including the oldest Stars and Stripes flag in existence) are two traveling inkwells that belonged to

38, 39, & 40.   The round traveling inkwell
(*opposite*) is covered with gray leather.
(The mosaic insert on the cover is separately
sketched.) Ink bottle is clear glass; both
covers are hinged and released by a spring.
Mark is a double eagle and "K.K.P.P." No.
39 is a tiny (1¾ inches in height) gutta-
percha bottle with a screw cap. At bottom
is a dovetailed maple traveling inkwell,
about 2 inches square. The little bottle,
slightly less than an inch in both height and
diameter, is closed with a hinged, spring-
released metal cover.

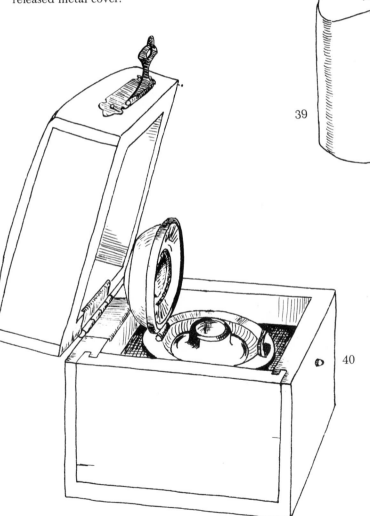

39

40

Civil War soldiers. One was carried by W. B. Cutting, clerk in the Battle of Gettysburg; the other was carried by George Kendall of Bennington, Vermont.

The historical association of such little wells makes them a fine addition to any collection. Ordinarily, the price for this type of well or for one of leather will differ greatly from the price asked for sterling silver pieces carried by an affluent traveler of yesteryear. One of our most costly traveling wells is of silver repoussé (embossed). Such a well was probably a nineteenth-century "status symbol"—professional men, ladies of means, and people of discriminating taste undoubtedly delighted in owning a mongrammed silver well, especially one presented to mark a special occasion.

There were traveling wells in which the upper portion was the ink container and the lower section a depository for sand; the two sections screwed together. Such a form would clearly indicate a mid-nineteenth-century date, when sand was commonly used as a writing aid. A round brass well of this sort with black-enameled body is featured in a collection we have studied.

For traveling at sea, a ship's captain sometimes had a boxlike desk of wood, which was often ornamented with brass or inlaid with other woods. Of rectangular shape usually and, although the size varied, generally about twenty inches long and twelve inches wide, these desks were equipped with the writing essentials needed by the captain and first mate to keep the ship's log. Some desks of this type that we have seen were supported by four wooden legs about two feet high, and fitted with one or more lidded wells of glass, which set snugly into compartments in the upper front portion of the box so that they would not slip about and spill the ink. Recently, however, a number of these desks have appeared in antique shops specializing in English wares, and so at least some of them are new arrivals on the American market.

The relief-decorated traveling writing case of brass that measures about 10 inches long and 1½ inches wide seems to have originated many years ago in the Orient. (The Oriental traveler could tuck it beneath his wide sash for easy carrying.) These cases were made in India, Japan, and other countries of the East and are seen fairly frequently now. We view them with a bit of skepticism. Recently we saw one that was a Greek reproduction and it was difficult to distinguish from the genuine old ones. The inside of this type of case is divided into two compartments: the longer compartment was used to carry a pen or brush; the smaller lidded compartment at the end held the ink. Other antique writing cases of similar styling are also seen today.

Of particular interest to many collectors are the inkwells that fall into the category of folk art. There are handsome ones that graphically reflect American life, especially of the rural areas. Some of these "folk art" pieces are tiny boxes cleverly dovetailed and mellowly polished, and precisely fitted with inserts. Undoubtedly a rural American would proudly carry such a well, perhaps the handwrought gift of a relative or friend.

Traveling wells have the same appeal as the small boxes coveted by so many collectors. Collecting them can be like collecting pages of history.

4

Clear Glass Inkwells

he biblical words "Look upon the rainbow and praise Him that made it" aptly describe the feelings of collectors of clear and colored glass inkwells. An assemblage of such wells dating from the mid-1800s reflects the light in colorful prisms and makes the collector grateful to the artisans who created these containers.

Elegant little glass wells are not only charming to collect but easier to accumulate and less expensive, usually, than standishes of equal quality and rarity. Through the years, so many fine glass wells have emerged from the homes of people of more than moderate means, to be sold at auctions or antique shows, that obviously they once must have been important household items.

Collecting glass wells is a more rewarding pursuit for the collector who takes time to learn something about glass itself. This amazing substance is as old as the earth—it was first formed in the fires that built the continents. Yellowstone National Park has an entire mountain of this first natural glass, or obsidian, a product of the volcanic eruptions of forty million years ago.

Man-made glass have existed as much as four thousand years ago, but its origin is obscure. Many researchers believe it was probably accidentally discovered by Egyptian and Mesopotamian potters, who first utilized it as a glaze for their pottery. We do know that the ancient Mediterranean civilization practiced all the techniques of glassmaking used today with the exception of mechanical pressing. The development of glassmaking through the various periods of history, however, was erratic, and early glassmaking techniques seemed to vanish with the centuries.

By 1291, the Venetians were successfully making glass, and by the sixteenth century they had reached what have been called "extraordinary technical heights." Eventually, these techniques spread from Venice to France, the Low Countries, and Germany, and into England. The English, in turn, carried them to the United States where, as workers were imported from various countries, glassmaking became as diverse in technique as the American people were in their backgrounds and traditions.

It is difficult to realize that glass is a liquid that behaves like a solid, for when its basic ingredients of silica (usually sand), an alkali (potash or soda), and some other base such as lime or lead oxide are fused at high temperatures, they—strangely—do not crystallize. The properties of glass change with the ingredients used. The mixture of dry ingredients is called "the batch"; when melted, it is referred to as "the metal." Basically, there are three kinds of glass: green, or bottle, glass, made of coarse materials with soda or potash as the main alkaline base; soda glass; and lead or flint glass, used generally for the finest wares.

Almost all glass prior to 1825 was blown by human lung power with the use of a blowpipe. A gather (glob of molten glass) was placed on the end of the pipe and blown into a bubble, which was held by a pontil or punty rod while being worked. The glass was manipulated through the use of such tools as pucellas, tongs, and shears, after which it was cooled slowly, or annealed, in a lehr (annealing oven). When the pontil rod was broken away from the piece of glass it held, the remaining rough scar, called a pontil mark, was sometimes polished away. Glass formed in this fashion is called offhand-blown or free-blown.

To give glass shape or pattern, or both, it was sometimes blown

41.   These clear, blown glass wells with stoppers range in diameter from
2½ inches down to just under 2 inches and in overall height from 3¾
inches to a little under 3 inches. They are heavy utilitarian wells, not
easily tipped over, which were made by various glass manufacturers
during the last three quarters of the nineteenth century.

into a mold. Body shape was obtained by blowing glass into a dip
mold or open-top piece mold, as for a wine bottle. Pattern-molded
glass was made by blowing or ramming a gather of glass into a
shallow or deep dip mold, or a part-size piece mold, with an intaglio
design cut into its inner surface. Blowing the bubble against the
patterned inside surface of the mold impressed the design on the
outer surface of the glass, which was then withdrawn from the mold
and expanded by further blowing. At times, for such articles as ink
bottles and bottle-type inkwells, a "Yankee gadget" called a snap
case (invented around 1850 and used until about 1860) was employed instead of a pontil, to hold the object for the offhand finishing of a lip, mouth, or other part, thereby eliminating a pontil mark.

The term "bimal" is sometimes used for objects (including ink bottles and inkwells) for which the snap case was used in the finishing process. Among the design motifs used for pattern-molded glass were ribs, swirls, diamonds, and other simple geometric devices.

To achieve both shape and pattern, a full-size piece mold was used. Glass objects made in this way are called blown three-mold because the mold was customarily made in three pieces, although two- or four-part molds were sometimes used. The mold seams on this glass are discernible. The designs used were mainly geometric, arched, or baroque.

The bulk of American glass produced during the nineteenth century, however, was made by mechanical pressing, a process in which the metal was forced into a mold instead of being blown into it. The molds for pressing glass were always full-sized, and except on low-priced items, the pontil marks were ground or polished off. This new method of glassmaking revolutionized the industry and introduced mass production, which resulted in the manufacture of entire sets of tableware in matching patterns and forms at low prices. This popular ware was called pattern glass.

Blown glass, principally offhand-blown, was decorated with applied blobs of glass (tooled or molded into motifs such as leaves or strawberries), with threads of molten glass trailed over the surface, sometimes in wavy ribbons, or embellished with crimping. Early glass was also sometimes cut, engraved, etched, enameled, or gilded. In the early days cutting was done by holding the glass against a series of wheels over which various abrasive mixtures constantly dripped from a container suspended above them. Engraving was done by a similar technique with a smaller copper wheel and a mixture of oil and emery powder as the abrasive. Cut glass has a polished surface, but engraved decoration is usually left unpolished. Etching is decoration achieved by coating the background area of glass with wax and applying a solution of hydrofluoric acid to the uncoated area; the acid eats away the desired pattern. Enameling consists of painting on glass with semivitreous colors, after which the piece is fired. Similarly, in gilding, brown oxide of gold or a gold salt mixed with a flux and with gum water or oil of turpentine was painted on the glass and the piece was then fired in a muffle.

42. Olive amber glass inkwell blown in a spiral-ribbed mold. New England, circa 1815–25. *The Smithsonian Institution*

43.   Blown three-mold inkwell, with applied decoration on top and body molded in GIII–29 pattern, was made at Marlboro Street Glass Works, Keene, New Hampshire, 1815–30. The overall height is just under 2½ inches. *The Corning Museum of Glass, Corning Glass Center, Corning, New York.*

Of special interest to the collector of glass inkwells is the history of glassmaking in the United States, for a good share of the specimens available today are of American manufacture. Some authorities feel that American collectors are too prone to want only glass of proven attribution, in the belief that it is better to have specimens that can be "labeled." Sophisticated collectors, on the other hand, recognize that it is generally wiser to acquire glass of superior quality and fine crafting, rather than to buy inferior pieces simply because they can be attributed to particular artists or glasshouses. Not that there is no merit in collecting only Sandwich or perhaps Mount Washington glass; but the collector should not go overboard in making provenance the main criterion.

44.   In the top row are four glass wells with funnel-type or depressed openings. The two at left are pressed glass specimens of the kind popular during the latter part of the nineteenth century and into the twentieth. Well at extreme left has a hole in the base and had a rubber stopper, which made cleaning easier. Second from the left is a well marked "BERNARD & FRANK N.Y.," which has eight depressions around the rim so that a pen could lie across the top of the well. Next well is blown. Well at extreme right, from Italy, consists of two parts, the bottle-like well and a separate flange with funnel opening. In the lower row, at left, are two pressed glass wells with plated white-metal hinged lids. The larger is 3½ inches in diameter. At bottom right are two square glass wells, the larger one (1¾ inches square) being cut glass with a separate pressed glass cover. The other well, also with a separate cover, is entirely of pressed glass.

45.   Six clear cut-crystal wells have lids of the same material, hinged with brass. Largest is 2½ inches square and about 3 inches in overall height; smallest is 1¼ inches square and just under 2 inches in height. The largest has a turtle imprisoned in the glass lid. The turtle is on springs and quivers realistically whenever the well is touched. All other wells have plain lids.

46.   Double inkwell of cut crystal is about 6½ inches long and 3 inches wide. The brass-topped wells have hinged covers. Black composition well inserts are marked "The Davis Automatic Inkstand./Pat. March 19th/ Oct. 22d/1889/February 14th 1893, New York."

The first American glasshouse was set up in Jamestown, Virginia, in 1608, and although it was a failure, this colonial venture has the distinction of being America's first industry. It is believed that only window glass and dark-colored bottles were made at the Jamestown glasshouse. Window glass was a very scarce commodity in the Colonies—English emigrants during the Colonial period were often urged by friends and relatives to bring their own window glass with them.

There are few records relating to American glasshouses of the seventeenth century, but it is known that several existed. Probably they also made window glass and bottles. During the eighteenth century, the most important glasshouses were those of Wistar, Stiegel, and Amelung. The Wistar Works was founded in West Jersey (later called South Jersey) by Caspar Wistar in 1739. It ran continuously until the Revolution and gave America what is popularly referred to as "South Jersey glass," which shows Dutch influence. The Stiegel glassworks, established by "Baron" Henry William Stiegel, produced the first decorative tableware in America. Amelung's glasshouse is said to have made the most sophisticated American glass of that period, comparable to glass then being made abroad. Opinions vary, however. Some authorities feel it fell short of the best cut glass made in Europe contemporaneously.

During the period when Stiegel, Wistar, and Amelung were producing glass, most of America's glass tableware was imported from England, France, Ireland, and other countries, as most of the eighteenth-century glasshouses in America were producing bottles. (Glass tableware was too expensive for the commonalty.) It is safe to assume that many American glasshouses also made ink bottles, for they were useful household items. Stiegel, we know, made such receptacles; his early newspaper advertisements list them among the items offered for sale. Many of the eighteenth-century ink containers were free-blown, small in size because ink was costly, and closed with corks. Blown three-mold ink containers were not made until later, from 1815 to 1840.

In the early 1800s numerous glasshouses were established in the Pittsburgh, Pennsylvania, area, and before long it became the glass center of America. Geographically convenient to the Ohio-Mississippi waterways, it was ideally situated for supplying westward-moving emigrants with household articles. A surge of patriotism had followed the War of 1812, and in 1824 American

47. The attractive cut glass well at left has a brass-hinged lid. Diameter, 3½ inches; overall height, 4½ inches. The crystal well at right is cut in Harvard pattern. The hollow bell-shaped base is embellished with a sterling silver edging of scallops and finely wrought fern leaves. The hinged silver lid is surmounted by a silver ostrich standing on fern leaves. Diameter is 4 inches.

48.   Cut crystal inkwell at left, with four grooves for holding pens, has brass collar and brass-hinged cut crystal lid. It is 4 inches square, 2½ inches high. Circa 1860. The pressed and cut glass inkwell in the center is in Cane pattern. The collar and hinge are brass. Well is nearly 3 inches square; overall height is 3¾ inches. The crystal well (*far right*) with a silver rim has Hawkes-type cutting of bows and flower garlands on the top, front, and back. Length, 4½ inches; width, 2½ inches; height, 1½ inches.

legislators passed laws creating high tariffs that made it possible for American glassmakers to sell their wares for less than imported English glass. Notable among the Pittsburgh glasshouses was the firm of Bakewell & Company, founded in 1808. It had the longest continuous existence as a glasshouse of any American firm.

As the demand for glass grew in America, other new glasshouses were established in the Boston area (the Crown Glass Company had been in existence there since 1787), including the New England Glass Company of Cambridge (1819) and the Boston and Sandwich Glass Company founded in 1825 by Deming Jarves. Jarves recognized the possibility of using pressing machines to shape glass and perfected such a glass press in 1828. This change in production technique not only eventually revolutionized the glassmaking industry, but also made glass more and more accessible to more people. The first specimens were inclined to have a foggy appearance, as a result of the contact of the hot glass with the mold, and the extensively used allover lacy patterns (1825–50) did much to diffuse such defects, although lacy patterns were not designed expressly for this purpose. Around 1850 the production difficulty was resolved, and thereafter a clearer glass could be produced.

By the late Victorian period, American glasshouses were turning out glass that literally "sold by the carload," including the colorful art glasses—Amberina, Burmese, Peachblow, Spangled, Overshot,

49.   The sterling silver and crystal wells shown here illustrate similarity of styling but extremes in size. The small one, about 1¼ inches square and 2 inches high, has a monogrammed separate silver cover, which fits over a silver collar on the well. The large one, more than 4 inches square and about 4½ inches high, has a hinged sterling cover inscribed "John 1909." Bears Gorham hallmark.

Marble, and the much-favored Satin glass with its frosty surface texture. The inkwell was just one of the hundreds of objects made of art glass by the various glasshouses.

Many of the clear glass wells of the late Victorian period were ornamented with etched, cut, pressed, or enameled designs, for those years were characterized by a taste for lavish embellishment. Engraving, the oldest form of glass decoration, was highly popular and, of course, appeared also on inkwells.

The technique of cutting glass is almost as old as that of making glass. The earliest cutters were lapidarists, who were delighted when they discovered that cut glass resembled semiprecious and precious stones.

The Romans are known to have cut glass as early as the fourth

50. Clear, cut crystal inkwell of the Brilliant Period with elaborate sterling silver hinged lid is about 3½ inches square and 3½ inches high. Base of well is characteristically cut with star. Note the grooves at the sides for pens.

51. Clear crystal inkwell with star-cut base, stylized swirl-cut sides, and silver hinged lid is 3 inches square and 4 inches in overall height.

century A.D., and glass-cutting techniques continued in use through the subsequent centuries, though they did not become popularized to any extent until late in the seventeenth century when an Englishman, George Ravenscroft, developed a formula for lead glass. This produced a clearer and heavier glass possessing a greater capacity to refract light. The glass also rang like a bell when struck.

The English and Irish cut quantities of glass during what is referred to as the Anglo-Irish period (1780–1852). This coveted cut tableware arrived here in considerable quantity. In her book *Cut and Engraved Glass 1771–1905*, Dorothy Daniel points out that "there is almost no early English glass in America which has not already been catalogued, or imported in recent years, and that Irish glass, while more plentiful than English, is rare." She further states that much more American glass was cut than was generally believed in the past, and that it has been cut continuously in this country since the days of Stiegel and Amelung.

Benjamin Bakewell is sometimes spoken of as the "father of flint [lead] glass in America." His Pittsburgh glasshouse produced glass tableware and other glassware that not only won admiration all over the country, but attracted visitors from afar to tour the plant. In 1817, President Monroe ordered tableware for the White House from Bakewell, and after his trip to America in 1825 Lafayette wrote enthusiastically of the beauty and superior quality of the Bakewell glass. The Bakewell company is known to have been making what its advertisements listed as inkstands in 1809. Because the company categorized these as ornamental glass, they were probably made of blown flint or lead glass.

In competition with Bakewell, the New England Glass Company, an outgrowth of the South Boston Works of the Crown Glass Company, also began to manufacture flint glass, and soon both this company and the Boston and Sandwich Glass Company were making cut glass. (The Sandwich firm is so well known for its pressed glass that its cut glass is sometimes overlooked.) These companies were manned by Irish and English workmen, who brought designs and glassmaking techniques with them when they came to America, so it is easy to understand why the New England Glass Company wares sometimes closely resembled Anglo-Irish items. Collectors of the New England glass at times have difficulty in differentiating between the two. Conversely, glass made in the Pittsburgh area contemporaneously is easier to identify, since its designs were strongly influenced by German glassblowers, who also brought their techniques with them when they migrated to America to work in the Pennsylvania glasshouses.

When the New England Glass Company and the Boston and Sandwich Glass Company were making cut glass, they had, as did other companies of the same period, separate cutting mills that frequently were located in different buildings. The New England Glass Company is known to have had twenty-four cutting mills for which they furnished hand-blown glass "blanks" (uncut vessels designed for decoration). Some blanks were for inkwells.

Other glass companies known to have produced fine cut wares were also established during the early part of the nineteenth century in New York, New Jersey, West Virginia, and Ohio. Notable among these was the Brooklyn Glass Works, founded in 1823 by John L. Gilliland. This company later became the Corning Glass Works, which through the years produced the finest of lead glass— plain or cut, blown-molded or pressed. It received numerous awards in its early years for the "pure whiteness" of its metal—its glass sparkled "like a diamond." This Brooklyn company also furnished New York City with the glass cups for its lamps.

The 1840 United States census showed that there were thirty-four cutting shops in operation in America. This substantiates the claim of many glass students that, up until the War Between the States, cut glass was produced in considerable quantity in this country, and that it was the economic conditions prevailing during and after the war years that accounted for the decline in cut glass production.

Some glass companies sold uncut blanks to firms that specialized in cutting glass. To complicate identification still further, some glasshouses sold their blanks to more than one cutting shop. The Corning Glass Works of New York sold blanks to various companies, including T. G. Hawkes and Company, also of New York State; the Pairpoint Glass Works in New Bedford, Massachusetts, supplied blanks to both Hope Glass in Providence, Rhode Island, and the Meriden Cut Glass Company, Meriden, Connecticut. Among the numerous kinds of blanks Corning supplied to Hawkes were inkwells.

Cut glass reached the zenith of its success in America during the Brilliant Period (1880–1905); the glass itself was crystal clear, embellished with deep and sometimes curved miter cuttings in such

52.   Three cut glass inkwells of the Brilliant Period, late nineteenth to early twentieth century. Many of the wells of this period were quite large, and some were cut in such popular patterns as Pinwheel, Harvard, and so on. Two shown here have hinged sterling silver lids, one with repoussé decoration. The square flat well is English; its separate brass cover may not be the original one. Inkwells of this period sometimes had separate cut glass lids made to match the bases, but we have found only one of that type.

53.   This photograph shows three types of cut glass bottoms. The wells are the same ones pictured in Ill. 52, and are arranged in the same sequence.

motifs as the hobstar, fan, notched prism, and single star. At the beginning of that period the country was just emerging from the financial depression caused by the War Between the States. More money was again available for nonessentials, and when the women of America saw or heard of the beautiful, brilliantly cut glass exhibited at the Centennial Exhibit in Philadelphia in 1876, they were eager to have the cut glass tableware and decorative pieces such as inkwells that they had been unable to afford for so many years.

The cost of cut glass, coupled with its popularity, motivated the makers of pressed glass to try to jump on the bandwagon by selling pressed glass blanks with patterns pressed into them that could be "touched up" on cutting wheels by semiskilled workers. This shortcut method of production soon flooded the market and resulted in a decline in the popularity of cut glass that was intensified when pressed articles ceased to be "touched up" and inferior glass was ultimately used for "near cut" and "pressed cut" pieces that were advertised even in mail-order catalogs.

Inkwells with cut designs have always been collecting favorites because of their diamondlike sparkle. However, the cut designs that appeared on American inkwells made about 1870, during the latter portion of the Middle Period of cut glass (1830–80), were simple, consisting mainly of beveling on the flat surfaces of the well body and faceting on the hinged or separate (loose) lid. Some were further decorated with painted, enameled, or etched designs. Cut wells appeared in numerous shapes—round, square, diamond, fluted, rectangular, hexagonal, and octagonal—and in single and double form; some were mounted in metal stands.

During the Brilliant Period and up until about the 1920s, cut glass wells were usually larger in size than before that time. Some were highly decorated with an allover pattern characteristic of the period—hobstar, buzz (pinwheel), strawberry-diamond. The bodies of most of the cut glass wells we have seen, however, have no more than beveled edges combined with a design cut on the bottom surface of the well to refract light. The majority of these wells with bottom decoration carry the single star or the Harvard pattern, one of the standard cane motifs.

Although it is worthwhile to learn the characteristics of the metal of each period of cut glass, most cut glass wells accessible to today's collectors appear to have been made after 1850. Many were

54. Group of 27 collectible cut crystal and sterling silver wells. If the collector must confine himself to collecting a particular type of inkwell, wells like these make a good choice. They were made in an endless succession of shapes and sizes with silver lids in varying designs. A group of such wells displayed in a cabinet, on colorful fabric, or on a windowsill sparkles like diamonds in the light.

55. Two characteristic Victorian inkwells. The pressed glass inkwell at left, 3 inches square, 4 inches high, has S-scroll feet similar to those seen on low-slung Victorian furniture of the 1870s. There is no identifying mark on the sterling silver lid. At right is a pressed glass inkwell, about 2½ inches square, 3½ inches high, in a drape pattern. The sterling silver hinged lid bears the Gorham hallmark. (Most wells with Gorham lids found today are cut glass wells.)

made during the Brilliant Period, but even these are now becoming much more difficult to find.

To determine whether a piece of glass is completely cut, partly cut, or decorated in some other way, collectors are usually told to ring the glass by striking it lightly with a pencil or snapping it with the finger. If cut, the glass should ring. This advice, of course, is of small help in inkwell collectors—the shape of a well prohibits it from ringing. The sparkle of cut glass is a better clue for inkwell collectors, as is the sharpness of the pattern. And because cut glass of good quality is high in lead content, a cut glass well is heavy.

Much has been written about "signed" pieces of glass. Very little nineteenth-century glass of any kind was marked; after 1895,

56.   Fine pressed glass inkwell (*left*) with engraved decoration has a monogrammed and embossed sterling silver hinged lid (diameter, 2¼ inches). Height of well, 3¼ inches. At the right is a pressed glass well with engraved decoration on four sides of the square base and also around the dome-shaped upper part. The well measures 3½ inches square, 2¾ inches high. Round sterling silver lid with pink French-type enamel is about 2½ inches in diameter.

however, cut glass was sometimes "signed" with a pressed or acid-etched registered trademark. The leading glasshouses of the 1895-to-1915 period generally put paper trademark labels on their wares rather than more permanent identification. The labels were of course easily washed away, and even manufacturers who bothered to etch a trademark on their wares did so inconsistently.

The lid on a cut well is often a *clue* to the period in which the well was made, but it is a far from foolproof way of identifying the exact year or sometimes even the period in which a well was produced. Designs were seldom exclusive to a particular year, and a temporarily discontinued style might be reissued later on. In general, the glass lids or covers (hinged or separate) used from 1870 to 1890 were faceted, although they might top simply cut wells with

57. The three pressed glass wells at left are in Swirl pattern. Largest is 2¾ inches square; smallest, 1½ inches square. Matching covers are separate. After 1875, this type of well was often part of a cast-iron inkstand. Cast iron was brittle, and so a great many of the stands became damaged or were completely broken and discarded over the years. The three wells at right (1875–1900) are cut glass and have hinged cut glass covers. Largest is 3 inches tall. Wells like these were often used in a silver-plated inkstand, and many such stands have also been discarded, leaving only the glass wells for the collector to cherish.

58. French pressed glass inkwell has intaglio-cut iris and iris leaves in typical Art Nouveau manner, on bulbous glass swirls. Diameter is 4½ inches; height, 4½ inches, including the mushroom-shaped, hinged silver-plated lid.

beveled edges. The Sandwich glass inkwells cut during this period were mostly simply cut, with separate or hinged lids.

Cut wells during the Brilliant Period sometimes had a separate glass lid cut to match the well. Most wells of this period, however, were glorified with silver or silver-plated hinged lids. (Silver, silver-plated, or brass lids also sometimes appeared on wells of earlier years.) Amusingly, a number of the silver and silver-plated lids look like highly embossed Byzantine (onion-shaped) church steeples. Others in mushroom shape seem to perch on the square- or round-bodied little wells like hats of rich design. Many crystal and silver wells bear the Gorham Company hallmark—"G" for Gorham and an anchor beside a lion passant. Fortunately, this company kept detailed records of its wares. The number that appears on a Gorham well is, at times, a clue to its date of manufacture. The Gorham Company has informed us that our wells with the numbers given below were made on the specific dates and were originally sold at the retail prices shown: D1858, February 27, 1906, $22.00; S3099, September 11, 1897, $13.50; S3211, December 6, 1897, $6.00; and S3213, December 1, 1897, $6.00. This data is not obtainable for all the wells issued by Gorham, but old records of this kind confirm the fact that crystal and silver wells were sold in the late 1800s and early 1900s as luxury items.

According to its old catalogs from the latter part of the nineteenth century, the Mount Washington Glass Works at South Boston sold handsome little wells of cut glass with silver lids, as did the Pairpoint Manufacturing Company of New Bedford, Massachusetts. Both were simulateously producing wells of the same design, so it is interesting to note that the Mount Washington and Pairpoint companies merged in 1894.

International Silver Company of Meriden, Connecticut, advertised wells lidded with gold or with oxidized (silver) plated metal. These, like the wells made by Pairpoint and Mount Washington, were most frequently square or round and about three or four inches across. New collectors may be surprised to learn that a miniature well can sometimes be a more desirable collectible than the same well in a larger size and is often priced higher than the larger one.

Many silver lids are monogrammed. Some monogrammed wells were probably very welcome birthday or "presentation" gifts, as is evidenced by the fact that they often bear engraved messages and

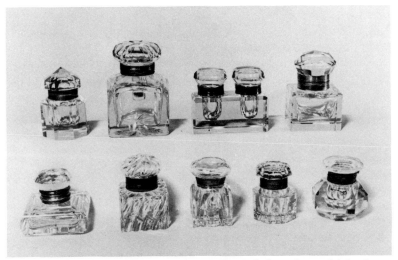

59. This group of small, clear glass wells with brass-hinged lids shows the wide variety of styles in which these popular nineteenth- and eighteenth-century wells were made by various companies. The largest well is 3 inches square and slightly over 4 inches high; the smallest one is 2 inches in diameter and about 2 inches high.

dates. A sterling lid usually carries the word "sterling," or a combination of this word and a hallmark, often just below the hinge on the band of silver that encircles the neck of the well.

Although not often found today, fine-grade crystal inkwells made in the late nineteenth century frequently had elaborate metal closures incorporating penwipers. A penwiper was a real convenience —the pen could be drawn across the wiper to clean it and prevent it from rusting after use. Also not commonly seen these days are the larger, clear, cut glass wells, usually plainly cut in a blocklike shape, often eight or nine inches long and about three inches high. They had two ink containers, probably one for black and the other for red. A type of smaller glass well had a hinged brass lid that opened from two sides to make "dipping in" much more convenient when used on a "partners' desk."

Most of the early American glasshouses that produced bottles during the late eighteenth century made "inks." (Though the Boston and Sandwich Glass Company and the New England Glass

Company sold "inks," these were probably made at the New England Glass Bottle Company of Cambridge, Massachusetts, which these two companies incorporated.) The "inks" advertised in newspapers by some companies or listed in company accounts were no more than bottles in a wide variety of shapes—conical, cylindrical, round, square, hexagonal, octagonal, and so on. Of crude design, they served the utilitarian purpose of holding ink, and today are generally of greater appeal to the bottle collector than the collector of wells and stands. William E. Covill, Jr., discusses these in detail in his book *Ink Bottles and Inkwells*, which—with its generous complement of photographs—is an indispensable reference for the collector who specializes in the bottle-type inks. Those made in the eighteenth century are not easy to find today, but others of similar type from the first half of the nineteenth century are available. The following types are perhaps more accurately described as "bottle-associated" or "lesser" wells because of their usual crudeness of design.

Blown Inkwells

Too little is known by even glass authorities to attempt positive attribution of these wells, which are commonly about two to four inches in diameter, or square, and about two to four inches in height. Extensive research indicates that they were made mainly during the late eighteenth and first half of the nineteenth century at glasshouses in New England, New York, New Jersey, and Ohio, as well as in England and European countries. Few had hinged covers; most were made to be closed by corks. Some were blown in a two-piece mold that had projections to form the depression for the well or for a well insert and also the holes for the quill.

This category includes also the flanged, round-bottle-type well with knob-type stopper, which has an overall resemblance to a scent bottle. It can be found in a variety of sizes. Made of clear glass with a heavy glass base, it has a more refined and simple beauty, probably because it was made up through the latter years of the nineteenth century. This bottle-type well was popular too because it rarely tipped over.

Pitkin and Pitkin-Type Inkwells

These little vertically or swirl ribbed wells, which sometimes look like tiny beehives or misshapen cubes, were generally made during the late eighteenth century and the first half of the nineteenth century. Contrary to what is often said about Pitkin and Pitkin-type wells, the direction of the swirled ribbing is no clue as to where they were produced. These wells were made at the Pitkin Glass Works in East Manchester, Connecticut; also, they were produced by the Keene Glass Works, Keene, New Hampshire; the Glastonbury Glass Factory, Glastonbury, Connecticut; and at Coventry, Connecticut; Mantua and Zanesville in Ohio, and New Geneva, Pennsylvania. However, as most of them were made in deep or medium tones of olive, green, and amber, as well as in lighter green and aqua, they will be discussed later in the chapter on colored glass inkwells.

Blown Three-Mold

This type of well was made from 1815 until about 1840. Some of the finest of these wells, which are usually under three inches in diameter, or of about that height, were made in either clear or colored glass by the Boston and Sandwich Glass Company. Most blown three-mold wells had pontil marks or scars and were made of colored bottle glass. The clear ones, which are of better quality glass, are rarely found these days. Glass hats were sometimes made from the same molds used to make the wells.

Blown three-mold inks are generally identified by the numbering system that is presented in detail in McKearin's *American Glass*, which divides this glass into groups according to pattern. In such a number as GII–18, for instance, the "G" stands for the word "Group"; the Roman numeral (II) is the Group number, and the figure 18 identifies a specific motif or combination of motifs within that overall group. According to William E. Covill, Jr., there are only twenty-three of these pattern numbers that apply to "inks."

Teakettle and Barrel-Shaped Wells

It is believed that the odd-looking, small, teakettle wells with a "neck" that angles or arches upward from the well base were first made in the early part of the nineteenth century. (The earliest were pattern-molded; most were made in two-part molds.) It is no easy task to attribute a well of this type to a specific glassmaker, since they were produced in England, France, and the United States. Generally, it is agreed, the French made the figural type. One French specimen in clear glass, about two inches high and three inches long, resembles a snail.

Benjamin Franklin was memorialized (as were other prominent political figures of his era) on a number of glass items, including a flask, platter, plate, breastpin, and an inkwell of the teakettle variety. On this last, a reproduction of Franklin's head formed the body of the well.

During the first half of the nineteenth century, glass became popular for making Presidential campaign "pieces." Platters, mugs, goblets, paperweights, and various other objects bore the likenesses of candidates for the Presidency and Vice-Presidency and their campaign slogans. Since barrel-shaped inkwells were being made in the United States at that time, it is thought that some may have been used to promote the election of William Henry Harrison during the 1840 campaign. Harrison was popularly known as the "Log-Cabin Candidate," and his mammoth outdoor campaign meetings and parades usually featured a log cabin on wheels with a live raccoon fastened to the roof and a barrel of hard cider by the open cabin door. The cabin and its accouterments were designed to emphasize Harrison's grass-roots origin. Among collectors of historical glass, any pieces pertaining to Presidents of the United States are prized, and so the barrel-type "ink" is an eagerly sought item.

Colored glass teakettle wells were made in abundance. Although they and other teakettle and fountain-type wells are not seen as frequently as in the past, they are still available. (See discussion under Colored Glass Inkwells.)

Fountain Inkwells

Quantities of fountain inkwells (they are not particularly attractive in the more primitive bottle-type form) were made by the "shut and cut" method—that is, by pressing in a two-piece mold that had projections (the plunger also had projections) to form the various parts of the well. Most of them were produced in clear glass in sizes comparable to the teakettle-type wells. Today, they are often seen as a part of a black-painted iron inkstand of inexpensive manufacture. Many, however, were patented, and they will be discussed in the section on Patented Wells.

Funnel-Type Wells

These commonly made little wells, which were both pressed and blown, look like sawed-off tumblers (many inkwells were made from tumbler molds). They appeared in this country early in the nineteenth century. Of a practical conical shape with a depression resembling a funnel, they were not easily overturned, and consequently were much used in offices and schools. For easy cleaning, some of them were equipped with rubber stoppers at the base of the well or with screw caps.

Pressed or pattern glass inkwells, which closely follow the designs of the more sophisticated cut glass inkwells, are also highly collectible. These pretty little cousins of the cut glass wells were made to appeal to those who admired cut glass but could not afford expensive, quality items. The first ones were made in only a few patterns during the last half of the nineteenth century, chiefly by the Boston and Sandwich Glass Company and by Ohio and Pennsylvania glasshouses.

Pressed glass, first made in America in 1820, was generally clear (infrequently colored) glass that was not of the finest quality. As already mentioned, the lacy patterns often hid glass defects. The technique of fire-polishing pressed glass brought it greater clarity, and then emphasis could be put on grace of form rather than surface designs, which—up through the 1840s—were heavy and simple. New manufacturing shortcuts brought about the development of ribbed and naturalistic motifs (bellflowers, ivy, grapes, and so on) for decoration, and American housewives began clamoring for glass tableware and entire matching sets in the attractive new patterns. In the 1860s William Leighton of Wheeling, West Virginia, developed an improved formula for a lime glass which, after

60. *Top row, left to right:* Crystal partners' inkwell, about 2½ inches square and 3½ inches high, is cut on bottom in Harvard pattern; brass-hinged lid is marked "Betjemann's Pat. No. 11049." Crystal well, just under 2 inches square, with cut-crystal brass-hinged lid, fits into a brass base almost 5 inches square. Glass well (1½ inches square) is fastened permanently into a honey-colored alabaster base inkstand (approximately 3 inches square); overall height is 2¾ inches. Cut crystal well has a green jadelike stone on the brass-hinged lid. *Bottom row, left to right:* Clear cut crystal well, 2 inches square, 3 inches high, has a hinged brass lid. Blown clear glass well, 3¼ inches in diameter and almost 2 inches high, has an embossed, hinged brass lid. Heavy blown-glass paperweight-type English well, 4½ inches in diameter and 2¾ inches in height, with heavy, hinged brass lid, is the type of well frequently but erroneously called a sea captain's inkwell. Tiny pressed glass well in Swirl pattern has a dome-shaped hinged brass lid.

the Civil War, was prolifically produced by western glass-houses. The New England glasshouses largely clung to the use of flint glass for their many products. Much quality glass, of course, continued to be made at the same time cheaper glass was being so abundantly manufactured.

Among the important makers of pressed glass were Bakewell, Pears and Company, McKee Brothers, George Duncan and Sons, Bryce Brothers, and the United States Glass Company, all of which were located in the Pittsburgh area; James Gillinder and Sons of Philadelphia and Greensburg, Pennsylvania; and the New England Glass Company and the Boston and Sandwich Glass Company in

Massachusetts. Though much is known about these and other firms, nevertheless attribution of pressed glass inkwells, especially of the earlier years, is difficult. In her book *Sandwich Glass*, Ruth Webb Lee pictures a bottle-type "clear glass inkwell, with Diamond Sunburst," one kind of pressed glass well made at Sandwich. It is known, too, that only the Boston and Sandwich Glass Company made wells (with hinged lids of brass or pewter) in both the Divided Heart (well-known in New England) and the Waffle patterns. They also made an inkwell in a pattern variation of their Standard Sandwich Star, in two sizes, 2½ inches and 3 inches.

Excavations at the sites of various early glasshouses, especially at the Sandwich Glass site, by such well-known glass researchers as Harry Hall White have revealed much about pressed glass. Perhaps future excavations will disclose information that will be of assistance to inkwell collectors and make the attribution of wells less difficult.

Inkwells of pattern (pressed) glass were produced at Ohio and Pennsylvania glasshouses in such patterns as Cane, Chandelier, Excelsior, Daisy and Button, Pointed Hobnail, and Thousand Eye. Most of the pressed glass wells in these patterns were colored, but some were made in clear glass.

Metal and wood inkstands, both those made in the United States and those made in Europe, sometimes had wells of pressed glass. The wells made expressly for such stands often have a base smaller in circumference than the body of the well, formed to set down snugly in the stand. Others, of course, are of standard square or round form, and still desirable as individual wells even if separated from their stands.

The excitement of collecting pressed glass wells is heightened by the fact that the collector sometimes discovers wells in variant patterns or unusual forms that he did not know existed. A friend of ours seems to have turned up such a specimen. Wells like it may have been made in flock quantity at one time, but this is the first one we have seen. There is a scalloped tray four inches in diameter, with a scroll design. On it sits a Swirl pattern well that has a matching unattached glass lid. (Some Swirl pattern pressed inkwells have matching lids that are hinged and banded with brass.)

Some pressed glass wells made during the last half of the nineteenth century combined clear and frosted glass. We have seen few of this type. One displayed at an antique show in New Haven,

61. At center foreground is a clear pressed glass well in Swirl pattern, with matching separate cover, that fits into a round pressed glass tray. The other wells (*left to right*) are: clear glass (Czechoslovakian) figural well in the shape of a Boston terrier (head is hinged and serves as the lid); threaded glass well with matching hinged lid; iridescent cut glass well with matching separate metal-bound lid; choice cut glass well with matching separate cover; square pressed glass well in Thousand Eye pattern with matching separate cover (this popular pattern was also made in colored glass); frosted glass dog (again, hinged head is the lid). The threaded glass well, 4 inches high, is the tallest.

Connecticut, had the charming difference of a tiny frosted finial in the shape of a bird. Figural wells of clear glass of the pressed variety were made both in this country and abroad. One from Czechoslovakia is a pert-looking little Boston terrier whose hinged head is the lid of the well.

Unfortunately for antique collectors, several glass companies have lately acquired the original molds from which old glass objects, including inkwells, were made. Thus, there are many reproductions on the market and more can be expected. These new wells are so like the genuine old specimens that identification is difficult.

In fairness to collectors, good-quality reproductions should bear permanent imprints stating that they are reproductions. Until legislation makes such marking mandatory, the identification of reproductions will continue to be confusing.

Studying a good collection of pressed glass, with or without inkwells, can be instructive for the glass novice, but it is of even more benefit to handle glass. Old glass has a certain feel to it—sometimes it is almost "oily" to the touch—and viewing is no substitute for handling. If possible, the new collector should find a friendly antique dealer who will let him handle some good pieces of various types of old glass. In this way, he will learn the sharpness of cut glass, the more rounded surface of pressed glass, and the shallow cut of engraved glass. He can also listen to the ring of flint glass or crystal glass and the thud of pressed glass of low or no lead content.

Inferior glass is often yellowish or smoky-looking. Under no circumstances should clouded ("sick") glass be bought. It is not worth even a small price, for it is in the process of deteriorating and cannot be restored to clarity.

The more the beginning collector of inkwells studies the various kinds of glass, the more he realizes how extremely difficult it is to tell where or by whom a specific inkwell was made. So many glasshouse workers traveled from factory to factory and carried their patterns with them, even improvising on old patterns (sometimes brought from Europe), that unless a well is accompanied by documents tracing it to its original owner or maker, positive identification is almost impossible to achieve. But identifying a glass well as from a specific glasshouse or glassmaker, as we have already indicated, is not of paramount importance. If a well is old, in good condition, not overpriced, and appeals to the collector, that is sufficient reason for adding it to his collection.

5

Glass Wells—Colored, Paperweight, and Patented

Colored glass wells of either transparent or opaque glass are the crown jewels of a collection. Although such wells were made in America during the eighteenth and the first half of the nineteenth centuries, it was during the mid-1800s and the late Victorian period, when art glass came into vogue, that those of more sophisticated design appeared in quantity and in rainbow array. These later wells have been the most accessible ones in recent years, and also the ones priced within the budget range of the average collector. Like all antiques, however, they are increasing in price, and now they usually are not only more costly than a crystal and silver well of equal age and size, but they are also getting harder to find.

Colored glass is made by adding various metallic oxides to the glass batch. Copper compounds produce red glass; compounds of iron make a bluish green; chromium oxide makes grass-green glass. Milk glass, on the other hand, is produced by adding feldspar, and, if only a small amount is added to the batch, "opal" glass is the result.

The New England Glass Company made a beautiful ruby glass by adding twenty-dollar gold pieces, which were brought from a nearby bank. This ruby glass is unlike other ruby glasses made during the same period—it has a golden glint in some lights. The New England Glass Company sold it under the name of Bohemian glass. Sometimes the ruby was overlaid on clear glass and a pattern cut through the overlay, but New England made items of ruby alone—for example, railroad lanterns; if the glass was chipped, they would still give a red light. Although great quantities of Bohemian-type glass were made in America during the mid-1800s (Austrian and German workers who were proficient in making it began working in American glasshouses then), we have never seen an inkwell entirely of this glass, although we have seen them of ruby flash and overlay (Color Plate 3).

Colored glass items are of four types: the same color all the

62. Arabic glass inkwell, circa tenth to twelfth century, is 5 inches in height. *The Corning Museum of Glass, Corning Glass Center, Corning, New York*

way through; two or more layers of different colors cased together
or overlaid one on the other; one color "flashed" in a thin layer on
another; and one color with a luster stain applied on the surface.
Cased glass is the finest of the colored glasses, old cut glass of one
color the rarest, and flashed the most common. Beautiful overlay
glass was produced at French and English glasshouses during the
nineteenth century. Whatever the color of transparent glass, its
clarity is always a most important criterion for judging its quality.

The new England Glass Company was noted for not only its
ruby but also its opal glass. The company made black, emerald
green, light opaque green, dark blue, powder blue, light opaque
blue, amethyst, canary yellow, and other shades as well. Oddly, this
company did not make amber glass. We have seen a New England
inkstand in opaque blue with dark blue mottling that has two
round, squat, ribbed wells. Doubtless a number of the wells of
opaque blue and of transparent blue that are seen from time to time
at antique shows and shops were made by the New England Glass
Company, although it would be difficult to attribute such wells to a
specific company, since so many glassworks made similar colors.

Deming Jarves of the Sandwich factory was one of the period's
strongest proponents of colored glass. It is believed that many items
made there in clear glass were also made in colored. Jarves was
especially fond of the deep tones of green and blue. The sapphire
blue made by Sandwich looks as if the color had been plucked from
a Botticelli painting. Sapphire blue was also combined with crystal at
Sandwich.

Museum curators and knowledgeable dealers are most reluctant to specify that a particular piece of glass is definitely Sandwich.
To be on the safe side, they call it Sandwich-type glass. For such
pieces, the collector should not pay more than Sandwich-*type*
prices. It is known that the Sandwich factory produced quantities of
colored cut glass inkwells in a wide range of hues, but the Sandwich
wells most avidly sought are of striped blown glass. These vary in
size from about three to four inches in diameter, and are not easy to
locate today. The stripes are usually of pink or blue glass combined
with white and clear. Striped glass was introduced at Sandwich by
Nicholas Lutz, who had come to this country from France after
working in the Cristalleries de St. Louis (1767). He was a master
workman in all types of glass but specialized in fancy glasses. The

63. Red opaque pressed glass inkstand, probably French and dating from the middle of the nineteenth century. *The Corning Museum of Glass, Corning Glass Center, Corning, New York*

64. At far left is a well of highly collectible and hard-to-find type —amethyst cut glass. It is a little more than 1½ inches square, and has a matching brass-hinged lid. The handsome cut glass well in the center, about 3½ inches in diameter, is flashed with chartreuse and has a hinged, dome-shaped cover of sterling silver. (This well was advertised in a well-known antiques publication; it is one of the few that we have bought by mail.) The octagonal cut crystal well at right has a cut ruby-red glass, brass-hinged lid that is released by a spring. Even the lock on the lid is embellished with a cut glass "gem."

GLASS INK STANDS.

65. Page from a 1920s catalog of Wilcox Silver Plate Company, a division of International Silver Company, Meriden, Connecticut, which was formed in 1898 by combining more than a dozen silver makers of the New England area, some of which dated back to 1852 and earlier, and were known to have made inkwells. Most of the inkwells made by Wilcox were of cut glass and had sterling or silver-plated lids. The cut glass was supplied by Meriden Cut Glass Company. *International Silver Company, Meriden, Connecticut*

Bennington Museum has a group of colored Sandwich glass pens made by Lutz that illustrate the many shades of Sandwich glass.

Walter Clemmons, an antique dealer from Manchester Center, Vermont, showed us a white opalescent glass well, approximately seven inches tall and three inches in diameter, with an applied transparent glass serpent of light blue coiled about the rounded body.

The Sandwich Glass Museum has similarly decorated glass on display and it is known that Sandwich made white opalescent glass. But to attribute Mr. Clemmons's well on the basis of such coincidental evidence would be hazardous, for other glasshouses made

66. Three cobalt blue embossed Carter's Master, or bulk, ink bottles. Bottles of this shape are known as cathedral bottles because of their arched panels. The small hexagonal bottle used for a smaller quantity of ink is also cobalt blue. *The Carter's Ink Company, Cambridge, Massachusetts*

opalescent glass and used the serpent as an applied decoration. Mr. Clemmons believes his well is of French origin.

Birds were also a favored applied decoration. Ohio glasshouses used them during the early 1800s to decorate the rims of Pitkin-type wells (wells with a swirled or vertically ribbed pattern), which have been seen in light green and amber. The Keene, New Hampshire, glassworks similarly decorated their blown three-mold well, which was made in amber, aquamarine, light green, olive amber, and olive green. As already mentioned, the Pitkin-type and blown three-mold, as well as the teakettle-type, are closely associated with bottles, but the deep-toned ones of colored glass make a worthy

67 & 68.   These two groups contain typical "inks" of interest to collectors of ink bottles. In addition to examples of irregularly shaped bottles, including three with off-set neck, the more common square, cylindrical, conical, and domed shapes are represented. Colors are clear, aqua, and cobalt. Markings are Caw's, Allings, Waterman's, Sanford, and J. & I. E. Moore.

addition to any collection of glass inkwells. Historically, they present a period of glassmaking when olive amber, olive green, deep amber, blue green, aquamarine, light green, and a few other colors were prolifically produced by bottlemakers. Sandwich glass authority Ruth Webb Lee in her book *Sandwich Glass* says she does not believe the Sandwich Glass factory ever made inkwells of deep-colored glass such as the Pitkin-type wells. Inkwell fragments excavated at the Sandwich factory site were at first thought to be Sandwich glass, but are now believed to have come probably from the glassworks at Coventry, Connecticut, and Keene, New Hampshire, where such wells were made. The fragments found at Sandwich, according to Ruth Webb Lee, may have been used for cullet.

Judging from the hundreds of colored wells we have seen, we believe blue to have been the favorite shade of glass for inkwells. Transparent glass wells appear in "electric" blue, peacock blue (a bluish green and particularly appealing), sapphire blue, and other shades. These wells were of numerous shapes—round, square, hexagonal, and so on. Some had indented channels in the glass to hold a pen. Usually there was a hinged lid of glass, although pewter and other metals were also used for lids. Cut glass wells of transparent blue green were sometimes made in a blocklike rectangular form in various sizes, with two wells fitted with hinged cut glass lids. Opaque blue wells range in color from deep blue to the light turquoise and powder blues. Many of the single opaque blue wells are of Swirl design and have matching hinged lids of swirled glass. Quilted satin glass wells in blue are especially handsome. Even a partners' well has been seen in this glass, about 4½ inches square with a patented brass lid that opens on two sides (Color Plate 9).

In addition to all the transparent cut glass wells in blue, cut wells were also made in rich amber and lovely tones of amethyst, deep green, and vaseline. Although cut emerald green single-type wells were made, we have never encountered one.

69.   The stand at top left, 4¾ inches long and 3½ inches wide, has a black cut glass base. The round brass well has a black glass insert in the brassbound hinged lid. At top right is another stand with black cut glass base, brass well, and hinged brass lid. Base is about 7 inches long and 3½ inches wide. In the bottom row are three stands of black cut glass. The stand at far left has clear cut-crystal wells about 1½ inches square with matching brass-hinged lids. The cut crystal "obelisk" between the wells, hand-painted with floral decoration, is heavy enough for use as a paperweight. Overall length, approximately 5½ inches; width, about 2½ inches. The two-piece stand at bottom center is grooved on all four sides to hold pens. The clear cut-crystal well, which fits snugly into a recess in the base, is tapered and has a pyramid-shaped crystal lid with brass hinge. Base is about 3½ inches square. The stand at far right is much like the one at the far left, except that the wells have crystal stoppers and the crystal obelisk has cut decoration.

Very few pattern glass wells were made in color. The most outstanding ones were of the popular Daisy and Button pattern—in apple green, vaseline, and blue. Daisy and Button wells are constantly rising in price, and are seldom seen these days at antique shops or shows. It is not as difficult, however, to acquire a colored Thousand Eye inkwell. Here, again, the blue wells are probably the most striking, although Thousand Eye wells were made in amber and vaseline glass too. Inkwells of Pointed Hobnail pattern were also made in blue. When made in the three above-mentioned patterns, the wells were usually fitted with separate glass covers, and at one time matching pen trays were made to complement the blue wells of Pointed Hobnail.

The white milk glass inkwells of this period are seen in both cut and pressed glass; pressed wells of opalescent glass were also produced but are not easily found today. Frequently milk glass wells are decorated with enameling or gilding.

The New England companies introduced art glass to compete with the cheaper colored glasses being sold abundantly by other glasshouses. The New England Glass Company at Cambridge took the lead over all other factories in making art glass. Much of their success with this type of glass was due to the ingenuity and skill of Louis Vaupel, an expert engraver, whom the company recruited from Germany. From this glasshouse came the popular Amberina (also made by the Mount Washington Glass Company at New Bedford, Massachusetts), which was made basically from an amber glass mix with the addition of a small amount of soluble gold. When portions of the glass were reheated, they turned ruby red and, if heated further, a fuchsia red. Thus Amberina shades from amber to red.

Burmese glass was developed by the Mount Washington Glass Company. Usually it has a matte finish. It was free-blown on the end of a blowpipe and shaped with tools; to achieve the quilted or expanded diamond pattern, it was blown-molded. Like Amberina, its color was deepened by reheating, the blush pink turning to a deep rosy shade. Burmese was joined by a long list of fancy and sometimes fragile glasses made by various glasshouses.

Although such art glasses were extremely popular, only a few seem to have been used for making inkwells. Some of the prettiest art glass inkwells were made of Wavecrest, a painted opaque opal glassware made around 1898 by the Monroe Company of Meriden,

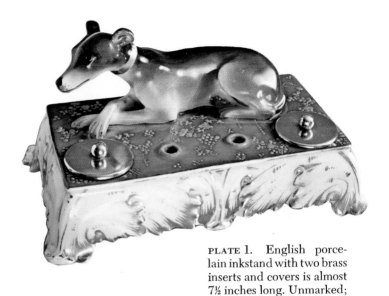

PLATE 1. English porcelain inkstand with two brass inserts and covers is almost 7½ inches long. Unmarked; late nineteenth century.

PLATE 2. Cut glass wells in vaseline and amber. Each of the vaseline wells has a different shape: square; round and fluted; six-sided diamond. All the wells shown have hinged cut glass lids. The tallest measures about 3½ inches. Wells like these were also made in clear glass and in milk, ruby, blue, and green glass. Circa 1870–1890.

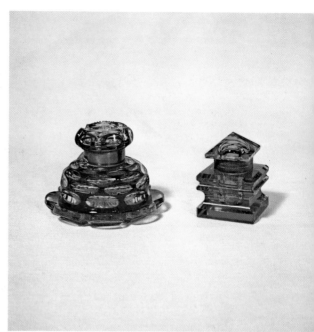

PLATE 3. The glass well with red overlay and a hinged lid is an unusual one. Diameter is 5 inches. The brilliant blue cut-glass inkwell, 2½ inches square, is also a rare example.

PLATE 4. The German majolica inkstand is 8½ inches in length. The well and the sander fit down into the stand. The two individual wells in contrasting colors are both Limoges, and approximately 2½ inches in diameter. All the pieces shown are circa 1890–1900.

PLATE 5.   This five-piece inkstand with attached wells is French porcelain. Elaborate inserts with a decorated flange fit into the wells and extend almost an inch above them. The separate covers (2¼ inches in diameter) hide most of the decoration on the inserts—this can be seen when the stand is in use. The tray is 9¼ inches long. Circa 1890.

PLATE 6.   The iridescent cranberry-colored glass and brass inkwell, 3¼ inches square, has an embossed brass lid with a stylized ram's head. The ram's head motif is repeated in the brass decoration on the sides. There is an insert of clear glass. The Loetz-type art glass well with a hinged brass in Art Nouveau style also has a clear glass insert. Diameter of this well is 3¾ inches. The handsome large well, 5¼ inches in diameter, with a hinged brass lid, ranges from green to purple in its iridescent coloring.

PLATE 7.   A particularly fine example of an English Victorian inkstand of gold-plated brass (1870). The edge of the base is beaded all around, but the cast scroll-like gallery extends along only the back and the front. The melon-shaped open-ribbed wells with hinged covers are decorated with interesting circular motifs; the lids are entirely covered with decoration. This stand, about 11 inches long, 6 inches wide, and 5 inches in overall height, was also made in brass.

PLATE 8.   This group of brilliant blue cut-glass inkwells (1870–1900) took a considerable amount of time to accumulate, as wells of this kind are scarce. The largest is 2½ inches square; the smallest, 1½ inches at the base. The paperweight in the foreground is also cut glass—wells and paperweights of the same material complement each other.

PLATE 9.   Opaque glass wells like these are rare. The largest, slightly more than 3 inches square, is quilted satin glass. The patented domed brass partners' lid is marked "Betjemann's."

PLATE 10.   The taller (3¾ inches high) of the two square inkwells is marked "Delft Germany" and has a matching hinged lid. The other square well has a separate cover and a white porcelain insert, but is unmarked. The Delft-like inkstand, 7½ inches long, has removable wells with separate covers, and is also unmarked. The cherub holds an envelope. European, 1890.

PLATE 11.   The 3-inch-square Dresden-like inkwell, with metallic copper frame-
work and copper decoration on both the lid and the well, is unmarked. The lid
has a copper hinge. The Victorian porcelain inkwell with hinged lid and unusual
yellow floral decoration is also unmarked. (Height is 3¼ inches.) In the center
is a marked Dresden stand, 9 inches long, with wells that set down into recesses
in the stand. Covers are separate.

PLATE 12.   In the center is a beautifully crafted 12-inch-long Victorian brass
stand with claw feet and openwork border. The ceramic wells with hinged,
heavily embossed lids are brass-capped at the base and fit snugly into recesses
in the stand. The predominantly rust and black well has a hinged bronze lid and
a bronze top into which a quill, sealing wax, and a sealer can be inserted. The
decorative marsh scene features flamingos and iris. Limoges, circa 1890–1900.
The oval inkstand in a deep maroon tone with floral decoration and gold doré
trim is pseudo Sèvres, 7 inches long. The lid is hinged, and there is a porcelain
insert.

PLATE 13.   Both the Meissen inkstands shown here date from about 1890. The pink-patterned tray, about 8½ inches long, holds two matching wells with separate covers. The smaller saucerlike stand in attractive yellow and floral decoration is 5½ inches in diameter. The well is not attached to the saucer.

PLATE 14.   The majority of the faience inkstands in this group are unmarked. One says "Sceaux, France"; another is marked "Aladin, France." The longest measures 6¼ inches. The smallest is 2¾ inches square. Late nineteenth to early twentieth century.

PLATE 15. In the center is an Imari-patterned inkstand with an Oriental mark, circa 1850. The wells are attached to the tray but have removable inserts with decorated rims and separate covers. Base is approximately 8 inches long. The white and bright blue reticulated inkwell, also Oriental, has a porcelain insert and a separate cover. The other inkwell, Royal Crown Derby, has a marked porcelain insert and a separate cover. It was made for Tiffany and Company around 1920.

PLATE 16. Staffordshire figural wells like these date from late in the nineteenth century. Those with dogs are nearly 5 inches long; the bird's-nest wells are about 2½ inches in diameter; the swan, 3½ inches.

Connecticut. The Monroe Company made their wares of molded blanks obtained from other companies, decorated them, and used the trademark Wavecrest (issued May 31, 1898).

One of the most important glasses developed in the latter part of the nineteenth century was Louis Comfort Tiffany's brilliantly iridescent Favrile glass. Tiffany's work was a colorful harbinger of "the shape of things to come" in American taste and the decorative arts. His creations, which included not only inkwells and inkstands but entire desk sets of metal and glass, repudiated the overdesigning of the Victorian period and introduced America to the Art Nouveau movement, which fostered free forms and naturalistic patterns.

Louis Comfort Tiffany, son of the famous New York jeweler, Charles Lewis Tiffany, grew up in an atmosphere of affluence. He responded with sensitivity to color and delighted in nature, once saying that he made "a practice of looking at the beautiful and shutting out the ugly."

After studying art in New York and Paris and becoming proficient as a painter in watercolors and oil, Tiffany turned his attention in 1878 to interior decoration. His first experiments in glassmaking had begun in 1872, and glass tiles were featured in many of his firm's decorative installations. Perhaps Tiffany is best known, however, for his stained glass windows, lamps, and his famous Favrile glass with its silky surface and deeply toned, iridescent colorings.

Robert Koch says, in his book *Louis C. Tiffany's Glass–Bronzes– Lamps,* that the word was taken from the old English word "Fabrile" (handmade), and that "Favrile" is actually a "Tiffany creation" to serve as a "unique word for the trademark of the Tiffany Glass and Decorating Company." (However, the word "Fabrile" appeared on some of Tiffany's earliest paper labels, about 1892). Within a few years the designation "Favrile" was being used not only for Tiffany's glass but also for his enamels, pottery, and metal items as well.

Many glassmakers tried to duplicate Tiffany glass, but no glassmaker was able to capture its full beauty, though several made lovely iridescent glass that could stand on its own merits. In Europe Johannes Loetz Witwe of Klostermuhl, Austria, produced iridescent glass that was very similar to Tiffany's. Loetz achieved handsome iridescent effects in green-blue-yellow, brown-blue-green, and in bold blue green, but his range of colors was never as broad as

Tiffany's and the surface of his glass did not have quite the same silken quality.

Frederick Carder's Aurene was another handsome iridescent glass. Some glass authorities feel that the beauty of his glass equaled the beauty of Tiffany's.

Other important iridescent glasses were made by Quezal Art Glass and Decorating Company of Brooklyn, New York, which specialized in more brilliant shadings of color; the Durand Art Glass Company of Vineland, New Jersey, and the Union Glass Works of Somerville, Massachusetts. We have not seen inkwells or inkstands made by Carder, Quezal, Durand, or Union Glass, but it is a good idea for the inkwell and inkstand collector to be aware of the various types of iridescent glass, and to have some knowledge of the makers' marks that were used. We have found that some antique dealers loosely refer to unmarked iridescent glass inkwells and stands as being "Durand" or "Quezal." Victor Durand signed his glass "Durand" inside a large "V," or sometimes with just "Durand" in script across the ground-out pontil mark; occasionally he used a rectangular paper label "Durand Art Glass." The trademark "Quezal" appears on most pieces of Quezal glass; and Union Glass Works' iridescent "Kew Blas" was usually so marked.

Most iridescent glass inkwells encountered by collectors today, however, are unmarked (except, of course for Tiffany's, which are not frequently seen). Unmarked wells of this kind are usually referred to by knowledgeable dealers as "Tiffany-type," although some dealers will refer to them as "Durand-type" or "Loetz-type." (Loetz did not mark many of his pieces, and although an inkwell may truly be a Loetz item, the dealer often prefers to play it safe and say "Loetz-type.") These extremely attractive, richly iridescent wells usually have hinged brass lids with designs in naturalistic patterns (Color Plate 6).

About 1910, the process of making iridescent glass became fairly well known, and cheaper grades of it came on the market. It was made in large quantities by the Imperial Glass Company of Bellaire, Ohio, and the Northwood Company of Martin's Ferry, Ohio. Gradually it was so cheapened that it was given away at carnivals and acquired the name of "carnival glass"; it was sold also at the five-and-ten. Flashed iridescent glass was also used for inkwells during the early 1900s.

Because of the great quantity of cheap-type iridescent glass

70. Rare paperweight inkwell of clear Pittsburgh cut glass, with typical Pittsburgh faceted edges defining the eight-over-eight panels. Housed within the clear crystal is an amethyst-toned goblet, which serves as the well. Diameter, slightly over 3 inches; height, 2⅞ inches. The genuine beauty of this piece is difficult to capture in a photograph; when held to the light, it is truly exquisite.

that was produced, before long it fell into disfavor. Even Tiffany items were scorned for many years.

Glass Paperweight Inkwells

Glass paperweight inkwells are distinctively elegant. In form, some of them resemble the spherical paperweights made as ornamental or whimsical glass objects; others are much like English scent bottles and have important-looking stoppers. They were made with various types of decoration, including spatter, devil's fire, and the colorful millefiori (thousand flower).

Millefiori paperweights were introduced by the Venetians in 1840. They were next made by the Bohemians, then by the French —the glasshouses of St. Louis and Baccarat and Clichy. It was probably inevitable that the making of paperweights would lead eventually to the manufacture of the millefiori inkwells that resemble scent bottles. In 1848, the selling company for the St. Louis and

71. Paperweight inkwells with controlled bubbles. The well at left, 3 inches in diameter, has an unusual hinged brass lid with a spring lock. The large well (*center*) is 4½ inches in overall height, 3¾ inches in diameter. The mushroom-shaped hinged lid is monogrammed sterling silver. The 2½-inch-diameter well at right also has a sterling silver, hinged lid. It is almost safe to say that these wells were made in New Bedford, Massachusetts, by either Pairpoint Manufacturing Company or Mount Washington Glass Company.

Baccarat glasshouses suggested that the St. Louis factory produce writing-table ornaments, including inkstands, shot-glass penholders, and wafer stands set on millefiori bases. Some of these items were in fact produced as a result of this recommendation.

The decoration in the base of a millefiori paperweight inkwell is comprised of cross sections or "slices" of cane placed in concentric rings, either carefully grouped or scattered at random. The concentric rings frequently encircle a cluster of cane "slices" and are often interspersed with latticinio (glass lace). The transparent glass stoppers, which match the body of the well, have matching millefiori decoration.

The English glasshouses at Stourbridge began making millefiori scent-bottle-type inkwells and wafer stands in the mid-1800s. Some authorities claim these were copied from the ones made at Clichy, for many French glasshouse workers migrated to the Stourbridge area and worked in glasshouses there. The millefiori decoration in the Stourbridge wells of transparent glass is usually comprised of five concentric rings of florets in red, white, and blue surrounding a central star-shaped cluster of canes. The colors of the canes vary; sometimes green, pink, blue, yellow, and opaque white are used. Like their French counterparts (which are also called inkstands), the Stourbridge wells have matching stoppers with corresponding millefiori decoration. Their overall height ranges from 5¾ inches to 7 inches.

French paperweight inkwells with millefiori decoration of the type described repose mainly in museums or in private collections, and are not usually available to the average collector. On the other hand, Stourbridge scent-bottle-type paperweight inkwells are seen from time to time at antique shows, as are similar ones with millefiori decoration made by White Friars (trade name for the James Powell Glass Works) located just outside London. The White Friars centers are Victorian flower clusters; their inkwells were made in at least two scent-bottle shapes that varied but slightly from those made at Stourbridge.

Closely related to paperweight inkwells are the paperweight wafer stands, or trays, as they were also called. These little stands served the dual purpose of holding paper in place and of being receptacles for the wafers of paste used to seal letters. They were made in various forms: some footed and bowl-shaped, with a

72. Clear blown-glass paperweight inkwell with matching stopper has green, red, and white glass ribbonlike decoration in both base and stopper. Diameter, 3½ inches; height, 4½ inches. American, circa 1890. *Collection of Robert Duplease*

concave cutting at the top in which the wafers were stored; others were large paperweights with depressions on the top surface to accommodate the wafers. Clichy produced a most attractive paperweight stand with a rounded millefiori paperweight base surmounted by a funnel-shaped receptacle with a hollowed-out top for the wafers.

It is commonly believed that the technique of making millefiori glass came to America from England, but the Millville, New Jersey, firm of Whitall, Tatum & Company rejected copying the paperweights made abroad. By using wooden molds, they created their own famous design—the large, blooming Millville Rose. In their scent-bottle-type inkwells with elongated necks shaped by hand they used a mushroom tuft in the body of the well and in the matching stopper. Several examples of paperweight inkwells made by John Ruhlander are in the collection of wells in the Wheaton Museum of Glass at Wheaton Village, Millville, New Jersey.

American scent-bottle-type paperweight inkwells are scarce,

and collectors who come upon any should be extra cautious and rely on the advice of a dealer who specializes in paperweights, to avoid paying a high price for a reproduction. The glassworkers who specialized in paperweight wells were, it would seem, most ingenious artisans. One of the prettiest of such wells that we know is made of Pittsburgh glass, amongst the finest glass produced in America during the Victorian period. It is shown in Illustration No. 70.

Of special interest are the wells supposedly used by sea captains to secure papers when they wrote on nights with the sea churning and the wind tearing at the sails. The curatorial staff at the Mystic Seaport Museum say that it was not customary for ship captains to take this type of paperweight inkwell to sea, as in most instances it would have been too lightweight and would have slid about. (See Illustration No. 60.)

The lovely little "bubble ball" inkwell with controlled bubbles in the glass was made in a variety of sizes and had a hinged silver lid of one shape or another. The precise patterning of the tiny glass bubbles in these wells makes them singularly decorative and probably the reason they were sold in great quantity during the late 1800s by two New Bedford, Massachusetts, glass companies: the Mount Washington Glass Company and the Pairpoint Manufacturing Company. (As previously mentioned, these companies merged in 1894.) These wells may still be found, but are seen less frequently as the years pass (Illustration No. 71).

Some dealers believe the paperweight inkwells comprised of a pyramid of iridescent glass balls were made at Sandwich, and they charge Sandwich-glass prices for them. Such attribution has never been documented, and it is not generally accepted. The collector should therefore be cautious about paying too high a price for one. We have seen a tiny one in this form in clear glass; it is much smaller than those of iridescent glass.

In the paperweight inkwell group there are a number of heavy glass wells with hinged metal (often brass) lids and also cut glass wells, which, by sheer weight, could properly be classified as paperweight inkwells. Those of blown glass are usually of simple, squat contour; the cut ones are impressively sized cubes, diamonds, and other solid shapes, which are frequently lidded with silver.

There is somehow a special thrill to acquiring a paperweight inkwell, whether it is a fine example of a relatively well-known type, a hard-to-find specimen, or truly a one-of-a-kind well made by some skilled artist in glass for his own pleasure. Although the last-mentioned type seldom appears in shows, shops, or auctions, the collector who finds such an unusual well can regard it as a treasure indeed.

Patented Inkwells of Glass

Patented inkwells of glass, either colored or clear, often were made for metal stands. Generally, they are quite plain, functional rather than decorative, but they possess great historical appeal. The important patented pump inkstands and inkwells of French origin and the Pairpoint Manufacturing Company patented silver inkwells are described in other chapters of this book.

The first United States patent granted for an inkstand is dated September 3, 1811, but in the succeeding years, the Patent Office has issued thousands of patents for inkstands, inkwells, and associated items such as penwipers and pen racks. Patents for inkwell designs *only*, including those for rubber caps with special filling features, were not granted until August 29, 1842. It is known that a patented inkwell appeared in 1851, but it should be pointed out that patents were granted for many inkstands and inkwells that were never made.

Among colored glass patented inkwells are the Jacobus wells imprinted with the words "Jacobus, General Eclipse Company, Danielson, Connecticut," patented May 14, 1918, with the trademark "Eclipse." As far as we can ascertain, these wells were made of green glass only, with a dome of clear glass as cover. They were made in both triangular and circular shapes. Sometimes Jacobus wells in single, double, or triple form repose on a deep green glass stand that matches the rich color of the well. We have seen one Jacobus well "glorified" with a silver appliqué, which makes it quite good-looking; perhaps it was a presentation piece (Illustration No. 74).

From time to time, a black cut glass inkwell appears at an antique show, occasionally combined with crystal. When such wells were originally sold in the latter part of the nineteenth century, probably about 1877, they were priced at two dollars. They were

73.   The black hotel-type cast-iron inkstand at the left, 5½ inches long, 4½ inches wide at the base, 5 inches in overall height, has a square (2¾ inches) pressed glass well marked "Pat. Dec. 11, 1877." The lid is attached to the sides of the stand. In the center is a round paperweight-type, heavy glass well with a hinged cast-iron lid. Diameter, almost 3 inches; overall height, 2 inches. The double hotel-type inkstand at the right has two 2-inch pressed glass wells marked "JUDD." The cast-iron stand itself is marked "PAT. NOV. 25, 1879." The well covers, attached to the sides of the stand, lift independently.

74.   The black cut glass and crystal inkstand at left is a Providence Inkstand marked "Patented Ap. 7, 1868." The stand still has its original tag with directions for use, and this refers to a "Rubber Fountain Inkstand with Pen Gauge Dipping Cup." The other three specimens are Jacobus wells, with dark green glass bodies and clear glass domes. The triangular well measures 3¼ inches. The round well at far right, better than 3½ inches in diameter, is marked "JACOBUS GENERAL ECLIPSE CO. DANIELSON CT. PAT MAY 14, 1918." The middle Jacobus well is on an almost square, green glass stand, 4½ inches by 4⅜ inches, which has two grooves for pens. The dome of this well is decorated with silver.

75.   Patented pieces (*left to right*): Inkstand marked "Morriset pen-unit, constant flowing. Bert M. Morris Co. Los Angeles Calif. Made in U.S.A." Inkstand marked "Sengbusch Self-Closing Inkstand Co. Milwaukee, Wisconsin. Pat. April 21, 1903. August 23, 1904. Jan. 15, 1906." Clear font, fountain-type inkwell, approximately 5 inches in both diameter and height, stamped "Pat. June 4, 1861, November 15, 1864" on the hinged pewter cap, has a brass weighted base and a cast-iron pen rack. The modernistic (1920s) stand at far right is metal, painted black with silver trim, and bears the identification "Robinson Mfg. Co. Westfield, Mass."

made by the Providence Inkstand Company of Providence, Rhode Island (the same company that made the well-known Plymouth Rock paperweight), and marked with the patent date April 7, 1868. The paper label still affixed to one of these wells describes it as having an "elastic reservoir." The directions (also preserved) for filling the well with a patented inkstand filler are dated March 1, 1877. Shortly after that date, the rights to produce this well and others similar to it were purchased from Samuel Darling of the Providence Inkstand Company by the Mount Washington Glass Company, which issued them as "Darling's Patent Inkstands."

Strangely, the "Darling" inkwells have much the same shape as the stylized black cut-glass wells of the Art Deco period (1930s).

Because of this resemblance, the collector should look at the under-side of the well for a patent date or mark. Wells of the Art Deco period, although presently increasing in price, are worth less than a well of greater age and of equal crafting such as the Darling well.

The patented phrenology-head inkwells are not often located these days—we have seen only one or two in our years of collecting. The head, of milk glass, bears an outline of the thirty-five phrenological zones; a milk glass font rests in the cast-iron frame, which also supports the head. This well was patented December 1, 1855, and is somewhat similar to one of graniteware made at Bennington, Vermont.

Certain inkwells evidently were patented because of their "tricky" lids or caps. These wells are highly collectible, especially when they are made of good glass such as satin or cut glass. Most patented wells fall outside this category—the emphasis was not so much on fine glass as on preventing the ink from evaporating or on permitting easy filling with especially designed assemblies, often of hard rubber.

W. L. Mason & Company of Keene, New Hampshire, made patented wells of amber, blue, clear, and green glass with hard-rubber cap assemblies. Wells with similar caps were made by the Burt Manufacturing Company of Akron, Ohio. Other patented inkwell makers include G. W. McGill of New York; the New England Glass Company (a patented well of milk glass shaped like a boat is a prized specimen from this company); C. H. Numan Company, New York; and the Sengbusch Self-Closing Inkstand Company of Milwaukee, Wisconsin.

Patented inkwells, as a group, may fall short of being aesthetically appealing, but they reflect the everyday needs of other years and the ingenuity of the designers and artisans who created them.

6

Porcelain Inkstands and Inkwells

*I*n times past, when letter writing was an art and hours were spent penning flowery phrases to friends and relatives, ladies' desks and writing tables were often gracefully appointed with china inkstands or inkwells of delicate decoration and charm. From period to period, these stands and wells differed in design and substance, but all were prestige pieces with feminine appeal. Those of the eighteenth and nineteenth centuries closely resembled the silver wells and stands that they rivaled.

Today, it is common to find the word "china" used loosely for all kinds of glazed ceramic wares, from true porcelain to stoneware. In strict accuracy, it should be applied only to porcelain of either the hard- or soft-paste type. Hard-paste porcelain is distinctively white, glassy, thin, and translucent, and it rings when struck. Soft-paste porcelain is lighter in weight and is a whiter white in color. It is also more fragile and easily scratched. When chipped or broken, two layers—the body and the glaze—are clearly visible; when hard-paste porcelain is chipped or broken, only one layer is visible; the body and the glaze have become one in the extremely high temperature used for the firing.

Biscuit porcelain (or bisque) with its soft mat finish is made of the same ingredients as hard porcelain, but it is unglazed. It was used a great deal during the eighteenth and nineteenth centuries for little statuettes of shepherds and shepherdesses and other romanticized figurines. Though it is a highly impractical material for the purpose, Parian, a type of unglazed porcelain made to resemble marble, was also used for inkstands and inkwells. It was made by Copeland (Spode works), Minton, and other English factories, as well as by the Bennington potters in this country.

Semiporcelain should not be confused with soft-paste porcelain. Lightweight, sturdier than pure porcelain, and less translucent, it can be classified as midway between ironstone and bone china. It was used in America during the late 1800s and early 1900s for inkwells and inkstands.

Bone china is another type of artificial or hybrid porcelain. It was first made in England at the Bow factory in 1748, and Josiah Spode introduced it to the Staffordshire potters. His son, Josiah Spode II, perfected an improved formula about 1800. This china became and still is the standard body for English dinnerware.

After molding, most porcelains of the eighteenth and nineteenth centuries, including inkstands and inkwells, were either decorated under the glaze with cobalt blue pigment, which was capable of withstanding the high temperature at which the body was fired, or enameled by artists in various colors over the glaze. Some factories sold a considerable quantity of glazed but undecorated porcelain to outside decorators. (In earlier years, Chinese and European porcelain makers had also sold glazed porcelain "in the white" to decorators.) Many of these outside decorators were highly skilled artists, and the work of some of them is widely recognized and highly collectible.

After 1756, some porcelain was decorated by transfer printing. The process consists of engraving a copper plate, inking it with a ceramic pigment, and transferring the design to the porcelain by means of thin tissuelike paper. This method, sometimes used in combination with the more common hand painting, was a less costly process.

A sophisticated outgrowth of transfer printing, called decalco-

76. Well-known type of Bow (England) inkwell inscribed "Made at New Canton 1751." Diameter, 4 inches. *Victoria & Albert Museum*

77. Nineteenth-century Chinese porcelain inkwell. *Courtesy, The Henry Francis du Pont Winterthur Museum*

mania, was introduced about 1860 for cheaper ceramic wares. In this process, designs in full color were printed on thin, transparent paper with special inks and then transferred to glazed porcelain and other objects. Decoration done in this way can easily be identified because it appears slightly raised.

The history of porcelain is a subject of great interest to collectors. Inkwell collectors, like others, will find it profitable to learn something about not only English and Continental porcelains but those made in the Orient and in the United States, because the types of decoration, the shapes, the glazes, and the quality of the body are all helpful clues when one must attempt to identify an unmarked specimen.

Most surviving inkstands and inkwells of the eighteenth century, along with the many from the nineteenth century, repose today in museums and private collections. However, it is nonetheless useful for the beginning collector to know about these stands and wells. Their form, style of decoration, the paste of which they are made, and the equipment on a stand are often an indication of the maker, place of origin, and the year or period when a particular specimen was made, especially since porcelain marks are not as dependable as collectors might desire. Marks on both English and Continental china often are lacking or inconsistent. In fact, Continental marks that have been in use a long time have frequently been copied.

It is known that the Chinese, down through the centuries, used porcelain writing caskets to contain their various writing equipment. To satisfy the European's desire for fine writing accouterments, eighteenth- and nineteenth-century inkstands and inkwells were made by such renowned porcelain manufacturers as Sèvres (France), which made both hard- and soft-paste wares, and Meissen and Nymphenburg, famous for their hard porcelain. In *Small Decorative Antiques*, Therle Hughes states that the Germans and French made "figure inkstands," which sometimes incorporated figures of "frolicking Chinese boys" or of milkmaids carrying yoked buckets that were designed to hold ink.

What has been called the "golden span" of china in England dated from 1750 to 1880. During this period, England became the greatest china-producing country in the world; Germany rated second place. Much of the china produced by both these countries was made specifically for export to the United States.

78.   Five-piece, dark blue Meissen inkstand. The tray is 8½ inches long by 5¾ inches wide. Under the removable pots, which are 2¾ inches in diameter, there is additional floral and gold decoration on the tray. The lids are separate.

From almost the earliest days of porcelain making in England, the Bow factory produced a soft-paste inkwell, now famous, which was considered a souvenir (Illustration No. 76). It was marked "New Canton," the location of the factory, and dated with the year of manufacture, either 1750 or 1751. This small circular well of unpretentious appearance had five quill holes encircling the well opening. Today, these wells are museum pieces. Lowestoft made an inkwell of similar simplicity in conical form, inscribed with the words "A Trifle from Lowestoft" wreathed with a floral decoration painted in underglaze blue. Simple cylindrical pots with floral decorations were also made about 1770 by Bristol and Plymouth factories. During this same period, Worcester made a circular well similar to the Bow well described above, in scale blue (so named because of its similarity to fish scales).

Ink, a powder prepared with water, needed daily stirring, and pens also needed to have the ink removed from them daily. Hence, most porcelain inkstands had quill cleaners. At times the quill cleaner was a casing that encircled the inkwell and contained lead shot.

As already mentioned, knowing what writing equipment was an authentic part of inkstands is a valuable aid in identification. It was not until the 1760s that the English made elaborate inkstands that included an inkpot, a central taper holder, and a pot for the pounce that served to prepare the paper when an erasure had to be made.

Early-nineteenth-century porcelain stands sometimes had both a pounce pot and a sand pot (more commonly called a sander). A pounce pot is also loosely called a sander, as pounce was often erroneously referred to as "sand." Real or "lily-white" sand first came into use with mechanically calendered paper during the 1790s. Interestingly, to conserve the sand or pounce, pots with large holes were popular; they made it easy to pour the sand or pounce back through the openings. Some of the pots without removable lids had a small opening at the bottom with a cork stopper so that they could be filled without spilling.

Because envelopes were not used during those early years, the paper was meticulously folded to hide all writing. On many social messages, adhesive disks or wafers were used as a seal. The adhesive was a mixture of flour, gum, or gelatine. A small, lidded wafer box was frequently included on porcelain inkstands (after 1840, it was used for stamps). During the Victorian era, a little taperstick became a part of inkstands, for the convenience of those who preferred to seal their notes more securely with wax. This might be flanked by two inkpots, one for red and one for black ink.

About 1760, Chelsea made elaborate inkstands in soft-paste porcelain. These elegant scroll-edged platform stands had pen trays with figural handles, such as a lamb encircled with flowers. The English were then very fond of porcelain figurines and figural knobs, handles, and finials.

Stands of porcelain and bone china were frequently colorfully decorated, with a deep mazarine blue or green being used as the background, and embellished with gold. Chelsea further trimmed these rich colors with gilded insects or with exotic birds on white reserve panels. The Worcester works produced small cylindrical inkwells with a scale blue background and inkstands with a pink

79. Pinkish orchid luster porcelain, snail-type inkwell at left has saucer-like base 4 inches in diameter. Bronze scrolls form the pen rack and the support for the revolving well. Marking is "Encrier J. L. BASGULE Paris." The disk between the side arms has a raised replica of a snail in the center; this disk serves as a cover when the well is not in use. Mid-1800s. The white porcelain inkwell at right, also French, is 4½ inches high and about the same in diameter. A clear glass ball-like reservoir (similar in shape to a light bulb) screws into the brass collared porcelain well. Marking is "Encrier Reservois P.B. SGDC Paris." The embossed brass cover of the font is chained to the brass collar of well. Mid-1800s.

background (as impractical a color as some used by other English porcelain makers for the floral decorations on inkstands). Chamberlain's Worcester featured inkstands with waterside and pastoral scenes on their trays.

The tray of one type of inkstand made by Spode is decorated with roses much like the naturalistic ones on Nantgarw porcelain—a ware seldom found these days—that can be seen only when the small wells are removed from the tray. Other makers of bone china encrusted their inkstand trays with flowers in relief or in combination with surface decorations. Two English factories particularly noted for flower-encrusted inkstands were Rockingham and Coalport. On one style of Coalport inkstand with characteristic flower encrustations, the finials on the two inkpots are roses. When Coalport inkstands were covered mainly with surface decoration, the ink and sand vessels were likely to be shaped like opening flower buds and to flank candlesticks of similar design.

Rockingham made a large and fully ornamented inkstand with typical flower encrusting against a bright green background. Undoubtedly, such stands were of nineteenth-century vintage. This company went a bit further than some of its competitors and used metal ink vases, which, as might be expected, had lavishly gilded covers. Trellis borders on trays were also a Rockingham design.

To add to the diversity of its wares, Rockingham also made toy inkstands. It can well be imagined that a young scholar would be enchanted by a little Rockingham shoe with a heel that served as a well, or would dream of dragons and kings when using an inkstand in the shape of a castle.

Minton was another English maker of china inkstands in various forms through the years. A bone china one of particular charm had three flower-decorated tub-shaped vessels on a rectangular tray. A single inkwell of tub shape, similarly decorated and set on a small tray, was also a Minton design.

The Derby factory traditionally associated with Japanese patterns produced inkstands in the Imari style of decoration, with its bright blue and red combined with gold. Probably most makers of bone china in nineteenth-century England made inkstands at some point in their history, for the demand for porcelain wares grew as the years passed. Today, there are quite a number of English porcelain and artificial porcelain (bone-china and soft-paste) inkstands and inkwells available to collectors. Because of their size and fragility, fewer of the larger inkstands have survived the years. When buying a china inkstand or inkwell, make sure none of the relief decoration is missing, and that there are no bad chips. Wells or stands with serious damage are not a worthwhile investment.

Among the desirable china inkstands to be found today are those made by Haviland, which are of a fine grade of porcelain. The Haviland factories at Limoges, France, exported an abundance of china to the United States. Their tablewares were extremely popular with brides of the late nineteenth and early twentieth century, for the dainty designs reflected the taste of the times. There were a number of other porcelain factories at Limoges, a center of porcelain making, and so the word Limoges on a piece of china is not a synonym for Haviland.

80. Porcelain wells: Hand-painted porcelain inkwell (*far left*) with spring-released, hinged brass lid is mounted on black-painted wooden base with brass stud decorations. Diameter, 5¾ inches; height, 3½ inches. The hand-painted well (*second from left*), about 2 inches square and 3 inches in height, has gold and colored floral decoration. Porcelain lid is attached with a brass collar and brass hinge. French well with three quill holes (*second from right*) is hand-painted in gold and with a green, pink, and blue floral design. Diameter, about 4 inches. There is a separate gold-banded porcelain insert. No doubt there was originally a matching cover. At far right is a Paris porcelain inkwell with two quill holes and a separate insert. A colorful floral border encircles this well. Diameter, slightly more than 3½ inches.

From about 1770, several small French factories made hard-paste porcelain called "Paris porcelain." Doubtless they made some inkpots and inkstands, but it is known definitely that the factory at Sèvres made a considerable number of them. During the 1850s, there was an almost insatiable desire for Sèvres, and this beautiful porcelain was widely copied. Many Sèvres stands of those years were ornate in design and decoration.

France was also noted for its "pump" inkstands, which were first made around 1839. On this type of inkstand, the lowering of a porcelain plunger forced ink into a porcelain font. When the plunger was raised, the ink returned to the reservoir. Such wells were sometimes made completely of porcelain, but as the most famous ones and the more decorative ones were made of combinations of porcelain and brass, this type of inkstand is discussed in greater detail in the chapter on brass inkstands.

During the eighteenth century, porcelain accessories for the writing table were made at the Chantilly factory and at the Mennecy-Villeroy factory, both in France. In Switzerland, porcelain was made at the Nyon plant, which is believed to have been established in the latter part of the eighteenth century or at the very beginning of the nineteenth century. It operated until about 1813 and produced only tableware and small pieces, including inkstands.

In Italy, porcelain inkstands were made at the Capo di Monte factory (1743–1821) and at the Doccia china factory, where "all manner of writing accessories" were made of porcelain. We have never seen a Capodimonte (the more common spelling of the factory name) inkstand, but recall one of Capodimonte-type that incorporated characteristic features—small figures modeled in high relief, lavish gilding, and bright coloring in predominantly pink, rose, and purple. Probably many of this sort were made.

Germany, too, through the years produced thousands of stands and wells, and many were exported to the United States at the turn of the century. At the Meissen factory in Germany, inkstands have long been made. In his book *Dresden China (Meissen)*, Egan Mew illustrates an early Meissen inkstand of Japanese styling with its original gold decoration. The wells are little Japanese figures with heads that serve as lids.

There were late Meissen stands similar to Coalport's tray-type inkstand from which it is necessary to remove the vessels on the tray to see the lovely bouquets of flowers beneath, on white reserve

81. This French porcelain inkstand measures 6¾ inches at the base. There is a hinged, gold doré-bound lid, and the holes for the porcelain-handled wax sealer and the quill have gold doré collars. The scene is in deep tones of rose, and green, blue, and rose predominate in the decoration over the entire stand.

panels. Such a stand is shown in Illustration No. 78. Its typically deep blue Meissen background is enhanced by gold decoration, although similar stands by Meissen were also made in lighter tones, including pink.

Late Meissen inkstands of smaller size were also made. Color Plate 13 shows a good example of the grace of even such small Meissen stands. These charming little pieces were made with backgrounds of various colors—deep blue, pink, yellow—and often are decorated with gay little flowers in white reserve panels on the inkpots as well as on the tray.

A number of the inkstands and inkwells Germany exported to the United States were "in the white," to meet the demands of the ladylike pursuit of china painting, which was a popular hobby here at the turn of the century. American factories also sold undecorated pieces of semiporcelain and porcelain for this purpose. No doubt many of the small, square, hand-painted inkwells with matching brass-hinged porcelain lids found now in antique shops were decorated by today's great-grandmothers or grandaunts, who practiced the genteel art in their youth.

A pattern book issued about 1832 clearly indicates that Tucker and Hemphill of Philadelphia manufactured porcelain inkstands and advertised them among the other ornamental objects they sold. Not long after that date (1848–55) inkwells were made in Greenpoint, New York, by Charles Cartlidge & Company. Doubtless quite a number of porcelain inkstands and inkwells were also made in Trenton, New Jersey, which has been referred to as the "Staffordshire of America," but such standard books on porcelain making in the United States as Edwin Atlee Barber's *The Pottery and Porcelain of the United States* state only that these Trenton firms and the Union Porcelain Works of Greenpoint, New York, made ornamental or decorative pieces. They do not specifically state that inkstands and inkwells were made by these or other American porcelain firms operating during the nineteenth century. If such American porcelain stands and wells exist, they may well be family treasures or museum pieces.

The china produced in the United States during the late nineteenth and early twentieth century was mainly semiporcelain. Much of it was unmarked, and this, of course, complicates establishing the identity of the makers. Here, again, knowing the paste, or what semiporcelain is, can indicate that an object may well have been made in this country.

During the twentieth century (1911) the Buffalo Pottery Company of Buffalo, New York, made what is called a "desk set" of the semiporcelain Emerald Deldare, a tray and two wells with underglaze decoration. This has Art Nouveau border motifs, plus a scene on the tray of two children playing with rabbits. This rare desk set, signed "A. Roth," is shown here and in Seymour and Violet Altman's *The Book of Buffalo Pottery*. The collector's chances of finding one of the Emerald Deldare desk sets is slim, even though it was a production item and authorities believe that many of them were made. (See Illustration No. 83.)

About 99.44 percent of all Buffalo pottery is marked with one of the several Buffalo pottery marks; it is also dated. Most hand-decorated pieces, in fact, were signed as well as marked, but earlier pieces often bear only a decorator's initial rather than his full name.

82. Ma and Pa Carter Inx were originally advertised in the *Saturday Evening Post* of September 12, 1914. The ad read: "Mr. and Mrs. Carter Inx—the little porcelain inkstands that made such a hit last fall lead the Carter line and bring to your desk a personality that will be an inspiration." These advertising gimmicks were given away with 25-cent coupons that were included in Carter's advertisements. They were first made in Germany; when production was interrupted by World War I, they were made in the United States. Ma is red and Pa is blue. Some ink bottle authorities say these little bottles may have been made in glass. Patented January 6, 1914.

83. Rare Emerald Deldare semiporcelain inkwell set made (1911) by the Buffalo Pottery Company bears the signature "A. Roth." The inkwell and tray have characteristic Art Nouveau decoration. *Courtesy of Seymour and Violet Altman, from the collection of Mr. and Mrs. Pat Cutini*

For centuries, the Chinese jealously guarded the secret of making porcelain. From about 1780 to 1840, however, they carried on a heavy trade in it with Western merchants or clipper-ship captains, who had found that Americans were eager to buy it. Much of this porcelain was decorated with westernized versions of Chinese motifs, for it was made expressly for the European and American markets, and the Chinese sought to please the Western taste. Chinese Export or Trade Porcelain is inferior to the porcelain that remained in China for the home market. Knowledge of all early Chinese porcelain entails lengthy study, and the beginning collector is well advised to rely on a knowledgeable specialist dealer.

For the inkwell and inkstand collector, there seems to be little available in nineteenth- and early-twentieth-century porcelain from China, perhaps because brushes and brush pots were the standard Chinese writing equipment, although this should not preclude the possibility that many stands and wells may have been made for export to the United States. For our own collection, we have succeeded in acquiring only one small blue and white Chinese porcelain inkwell (see Color Plate 15). Because of the pierced or weblike design in the porcelain, this type of ware is sometimes referred to as "reticulated" by those who deal in Oriental antiques.

In their early years of porcelain making, the Japanese copied the Chinese. The majority of Japanese porcelain seen outside Japan was made specifically for export. One of Japan's best-known export porcelains in the West is Imari, which is generally decorated with a mixture of flowers, scrolls, and panels in dark blue, red, and gold painted on a heavy bluish-toned body. This ware was made in Japan as early as 1650, and bears the name of the port near Arita from which it was shipped. The first Imari was brought to Colonial America by Dutch traders, but the great bulk of it imported into the United States from Japan arrived during the 1875–95 period. Imari has been copied through the years by both the Chinese and English, and so there is sometimes difficulty in identifying a specimen. It can also be confused with Gaudy Dutch pottery, which has bold Imari-type designs and coloring. An Imari-patterned inkstand in our collection (Color Plate 15) may be just one of many made exactly alike, but it is the only one we have found. It was sold to us as Japanese, but we are not sure of its origin.

Of recently aroused interest is "Hand-painted Nippon," generally a fine grade of porcelain, much of it tastefully decorated and often embellished with gold. Desk sets of Hand-painted Nippon— sometimes consisting of as many as six pieces—were made in considerable variety. One with a dark-toned satin finish consists of a small rectangular tray with separate inkpot; probably it is representative of many of its kind. In the typical restrained Japanese fashion, the tray is decorated with but one butterfly, as is the inkwell. Small single wells of Hand-painted Nippon can also be found from time to time, but some of these may have been desk-set items. One such well, about 2½ inches square and 3 inches high, is decorated with hand-painted designs in tan and jade green and highlighted with gold.

In addition to the countries previously mentioned, hard-paste porcelain was made in Austria, Holland, and elsewhere, and soft-paste in Switzerland, Belgium, and Denmark, to name just a few.

The histories of the various factories that produced porcelain and artificial porcelain are generally engrossing, filled with colorful legends and little-known facts. To become knowledgeable about the marks used on all these porcelains requires extensive study. Many factories used more than just one or two marks. Chelsea had its Red Anchor period, when it produced a superior porcelain, but it also had a Gold Anchor period. Meissen used a variety of marks, which were prolifically imitated by other firms. It is easy to see why there are entire books on pottery and porcelain marks. All collectors will find it useful to own a book of marks for ready reference, though no one book can be expected to contain every mark that was ever used.

Porcelain was also employed for making the inserts used for inkstands and inkwells of materials other than china, such as brass, bronze, and wood. These days, the inserts are often found chipped or cracked, but this need not deter one from buying a stand or well that is otherwise in good condition and a desirable acquisition.

Part of the fun of collecting porcelain and artificial porcelain inkwells and stands lies in the fact that specimens of unexpected style and decoration, or bearing unfamiliar marks, are constantly turning up in antique shops and shows.

7

Pottery Inkstands and Inkwells

*T*he whimsically appealing Staffordshire figural inkstand, the classically beautiful stand of Wedgwood basalt, and the French faience inkwell with its genre charm reflect the diversity of design, form, and texture to be found in pottery inkstands and inkwells. They are intimately related to the periods of history in which they were made and the people who created them, and doubtless they colorfully fulfilled the needs of those who could not afford fine china but enjoyed owning "next best."

Pottery, by definition, includes all wares made of clay and baked—unglazed or glazed, including hard nonporous stoneware and soft-paste, porous earthenware, of which most American household crockery is made. It is distinguished from translucent porcelain by the fact that it is opaque when held to the light, and most often is made from colored clays. When fired at different temperatures with a glaze, the clay and the glaze do not combine. Earthenware, the largest pottery group, includes among its types faience, majolica, delft, and creamware.

Pottery making is an art that has been practiced in just about every country and during every era since prehistoric times. In the eighteenth century the earthenwares that had been made for so many centuries were advanced to a new height by Josiah Wedgwood's perfection of off-white creamware. Meanwhile, in America, Colonial potters began using local clay to satisfy their pottery needs, which, even in those early years, must have included primitively shaped ink containers. Examples exist of many types of early pottery from just about every period, but of course most early specimens are in museums and private collections. Among these are very few examples of American-made pottery dating before 1700, as very little pottery was made prior to that date.

84. Four-part French faience inkstand marked "SX France." Tray is about 6½ inches square; well has four quill holes and is 3 inches square. There is a separate insert of the same material for ink and a separate lid. Decoration on the white ground consists of green roses, mulberry striping, a scene with castles on one side and with cottages on the other, also in mulberry.

In France, during the sixteenth century, the making of earthenware, guided by Bernard Palissy, was elevated to a new high level, and at the oldest French faience factory, which was located in Rouen, a number of inkstands were made. Some of these stands give evidence of this factory's famous polychrome decoration in Chinese style, like the stand in the Cluny Museum. The Rouen factory also was well known for its en rocaille decoration, which included quivers and flaming torches in polychrome.

In Lunéville, other highly interesting inkstands were made imitating the popular Strasbourg style of china. One such surviving stand has the scroll-type platform base seen in the inkstands of numerous factories in the eighteenth and nineteenth centuries. This particular Lunéville stand is described as having "nozzels and a watchstand," which were Strasbourg features. Similar stands were made at the French Rennes factory, one of which, painted in blue and yellow, is in the Sèvres Museum.

French faience inkwells and inkstands are seen today from time to time. Those of simple form are classified more properly as inkwells. They probably were made during the nineteenth century, but are colorful and pretty examples of this type of pottery. (See Illustration No. 84.)

Important pottery stands resembled those made of silver. French potters, like their fellow artisans in other countries, followed the lines of the silver inkstands of other periods, including the baroque, rococo, and neoclassical.

France produced other types of pottery inkwells as well as redware pottery ink bottles, which were popular in this country because they contained a high-grade ink. Little attention has been given to the twentieth-century French inkwells and inkstands of varying sizes made by the Henriot factory of Quimper (pronounced kam-pair) of Finistère, France. They, too, deserve to be mentioned, for they are attractive additions to any collection. These appealing little pieces, which arrived in this country from about 1900 to 1921, are gaily decorated with Breton figures in bright coloring on grounds of white, cream, yellow, and sometimes other colors. Some are simply contoured single wells or unadorned stands with two vessels for ink.

The majority of small faience inkwells immediately suggest the word pottery, for they are of plain form and gay design, often being

85. Spanish faience inkpots: The example at left dates from early in the
eighteenth century. It is decorated in the Talavera manner with a hound
in a landscape setting, and also depicts birds in flight. The cover is
decorated in matching style. Unidentified mark. Diameter of well, 3
inches. At the right is a twentieth-century copy of the eighteenth-century
well. Mark is "YC Mallorga."

circular with a central well and quill holes for inserting the quills
into a dry chamber surrounding the well itself. Some of them, but
not all, have a marking on the bottom, and if imported into this
country after 1891, they have, in accordance with the McKinley
tariff laws, the country of origin marked or, possibly, impressed on
them. Many such wells, even stands, of faience have vague markings that almost defy identification. (Faience markings, like so many
others, require special study.)

The Portuguese and Spanish made faience, and a small round
well about three inches in diameter in our own collection has been
identified as being Spanish or Portuguese, early eighteenth century
(Illustration No. 85). It is marked, but because of the difficulty of
deciphering the vague brushstrokes, the appraiser would not hazard
a more precise identification.

In Italy there was widespread production of majolica by the
middle of the fifteenth century, and Italian majolica (today often
called faience) became a highly integrated part of Renaissance art.
An Italian majolica inkstand in the Boston Museum of Fine Arts

86. This extremely rare majolica inkstand (circa 1500), from the famous collection of the Marchese d'Azeglio Passavant and Jacob Goldschmit, is a fine example of Italian Renaissance majolica work as a fully developed craft. It was probably made by Giovanni Maria at Castel Durante or Faenza, Italy. *Courtesy, Museum of Fine Arts, Boston*

collection clearly shows the way sixteenth-century Italian potters, working in the majolica centers around Faenza, sought to express high levels of artistry in faience—even in so domesic an article as an inkstand. Believed probably to have been made in Faenza by Giovanni Maria, it has firm architectural lines and bold pictorial decoration. Obviously, it commemorates a personal occasion, for a medallion in the center has two clasped hands with inscribed scrolls that read: "I give you my hand. Give me your fidelity." The words may represent the marriage promise of the couple portrayed (by two portrait busts) at the sides of the well. This stand is predominantly deep blue and light amber brown, and the glaze gives the piece a porcelainlike surface.

Many of the inkstands and inkwells of German manufacture with a delft-type decoration (usually blue and white) that are available today are of fine china. This should be kept in mind when buying delft-type ware marked "Delft," for it is not at all like the earthenware product from Holland called "Delft," which has a nonporous surface from having been dipped into a tin glaze or tin enamel. When an object was fired, this glaze became an opaque milk-white coating, which was decorated with painted designs in various colors but most often in shades of blue and purple.

As England was the largest china-producing country during the nineteenth century, pottery inkstands and inkwells as well as those of porcelain were of course made and often exported. A considerable variety of them is available today for collectors. They range from ordinary little redware wells with black glaze, hinged lids, and overall half-spherical shape, to Victorian-looking inkstands of yellow with two ink vessels, to handsome, imposing stands of basalt. Even pottery ink bottles were made and, in competition with France, were shipped to the United States because they too held a superior grade of ink. Some of these bottles, many of which were of stoneware and redware, were made by J. Bourne of Denby and P. & J. Arnold of London. The glaze on most bottles varied from light to dark brown; others had a grayish white glaze; the majority of the glazes were shiny.

No name in England's long history of ceramic art is more honored or widely known than that of Josiah Wedgwood (1730–95). In 1754, at the age of twenty-four, he became Thomas Whieldon's junior partner. This was a high distinction for such a young man, as Whieldon was the most important potter in Staffordshire.

87. Rare Gaudy Ironstone stand with a conglomeration of vivid designs and colors (predominantly deep blue and green, and orange) is 9½ inches long at the base and 5 inches wide. There are two removable wells with separate covers and an attached wafer box with separate cover. Circa 1880. Although unmarked, it is of English origin.

88. The brown glazed pottery ink bottles at left range in size from 7½ inches tall with a diameter of about 3 inches, to 5 inches tall with a diameter just under 2½ inches. At right are three small brown glazed pottery ink bottles. Conical one is about 2½ inches in height; the middle one is 2¼ inches, and the one at right is just under 2 inches in height. Probably English or American in origin.

89. The three blackware wells in the top row are about 2¾ inches, 2½ inches, and 3½ inches in diameter, respectively. The three-compartmented redware inkwell at bottom left has a brown glaze. One section is for sand. The well has a clear-glass blown insert. The well at bottom center with funnel-type opening has brown glaze over a yellowish pottery base. Top diameter is slightly more than 3 inches; height, 2½ inches. There are ten panels around the base. At far right is another, somewhat smaller well with brown glaze (tan pottery base) with funnel-type opening. This well also has ten panels around the base.

He made all types of pottery—red stoneware, salt glaze, and, in particular, multicolored glazes. During their five-year partnership, Wedgwood and Whieldon experimented individually. This freedom to experiment and his association with Whieldon probably led Wedgwood to the eventual perfecting of creamware, a creamy white lead-glazed earthenware resembling porcelain, which he called Queen's ware. However, creamware was not invented by Wedgwood. It had been introduced in England in 1725 by Thomas Astbury, and later also made by Whieldon and other English potters. Wedgwood began the manufacture of creamware in 1759/60, but did not supply it in quantity until 1765. It revolutionized the potter's trade and made earthenware popular for daily table use. Wolf Mankowitz says in his book *Wedgwood* that every conceivable type of useful ware was made from it, and surely inkwells and stands were included.

Josiah Wedgwood made a number of types of inkstands and wells. As early as the period of the Wedgwood and Bentley partnership (1768–80), a drum-shaped well of basalt (fine-grained, unglazed, black stoneware, a refinement of an earlier Egyptian black) with holes for quills was made. Wells of this shape in blackware were also made by Neale & Company, Elijah Mayer, and John Turner of Lane End (Staffordshire), as well as other potters. Some of these wells are decorated with reeding and fluting. (See Illustration No. 89.) Happily, small blackware inkwells can be found today at moderate prices.

Many pieces of Wedgwood are marked "Wedgwood"; the initials "W & B" (used during the Wedgwood and Bentley period) may also be encountered on this ware. A thorough study of Wedgwood marks is helpful in pinpointing the age of the object. Be warned that when a second "e" appears in the name Wedgwood, or "& Co." is added to the name, or the letters "D" and "G" are transposed, entirely different makers are indicated.

In 1779, a London trade catalog of Wedgwood and Bentley listed ink receptacles among the ornamental wares sold, along with eye cups and paint chests. The inkwell advertised was of black jasper, simple in contour, fairly conical, and designed to counteract the evaporation of ink by means of including several chambers. Jasper has a fine crystalline body, and the 1779 advertisement claimed that it "never corrodes with the ink or absorbs it." Jasper is colored by the addition of various oxides—cobalt for blue, and so on. It brought much fame to Wedgwood; thousands of relief portraits, plaques, and vases, as well as countless other items, were made from it. The most familiar jasperware is the blue, but it was made in pale shades of yellow, lilac, and green as well. Wedgwood also made a red stoneware called Rosso Antico, which he considered a "cheaper" ware; it was used effectively for relief decoration during this period (1776–86). A desk set of jasperware was decorated with a relief of children playing.

To rival the silver inkstands of the 1800s, Josiah Wedgwood II shrewdly produced black basalt stands with Egyptian designs for gentlemen's desks—they were not as effeminate-looking as the porcelain stands were. A fine example of such a stand can be seen in Wolf Mankowitz's book *Wedgwood*. This boat-shaped basalt (stoneware) inkstand—its fine compact black body resembles the Egyptian marble for which it was named—is characteristically decorated with applied scarab beetles, lotus flowers, and other Egyptian motifs. It was probably a great favorite during the early nineteenth century, when classical designs were emphasized.

At the other end of the English pottery spectrum are the Staffordshire figural inkwells. Owning one of these little earthenware figures is like having a permanent piece of childhood in your possession. Colorful reclining dogs, swans reposing beneath palm trees, and the other similar delightful figures that adorn these English wells have a storybook appeal.

Generally speaking, the name "Staffordshire" does not apply to a particular type of ware. It refers to a county in England where ceramics have been made since Roman times. It was there that the transfer-printed wares of the 1800s, today commonly referred to as "Staffordshire," were produced in large quantities for an eager American market by such famous English potters as Enoch Wood, Adams, Clews, the Ridgways, and Jackson. Staffordshire pottery includes slip-decorated and salt-glazed wares, redware, creamware, and the coarse pottery decorated with bright colors from which the crudely modeled "cottage pieces" were made. Enoch Wood and Ralph Wood, peers of English pottery, modeled a few "cottage pieces" of finer quality, but a goodly number of the Staffordshire pieces seen today are of white earthenware, made throughout the mid-1800s and originally sold for just a few shillings.

In spite of their crudeness, these "cottage pieces" (which include inkwells) are gay and spirited-looking little rustic groupings of such figures as shepherds and shepherdesses and, of course, the popular swans resting in the shade of a tree. Made by fairly unskilled workers to attract the attention of the "cottager" of rural England, they were priced just high enough to make them desirable to own, but not too high to be beyond the purse of the farmer whose wife coveted one. They sold as popularly in England then as "fish and chips" do today.

The first of these Staffordshire pieces were made during the early 1800s; they were reproduced later in the century with less attention to detail and with somewhat duller colors. However, many seen today in antique shops were reproduced not more than fifty or sixty years ago. We are not at all averse to collecting inkwells produced then or even a bit later; to us they are thoroughly collectible items. But, because these recent reproductions of Staffordshire inkwells are on the market, it is best to buy such inkwells (they are sometimes called stands) from a knowledgeable dealer who has some certainty of the age of a particular specimen or possesses documentation about it. A dealer who specializes in Staffordshire earthenware can provide much-needed expertise to guide you in your selection—differentiating the old Staffordshire figural wells from the new by such factors as the absence or presence of a concave bottom, for instance, can be a most unreliable method. Some people claim they can tell by the feel of the glaze on Staffordshire hounds and other figures whether a piece is old or new. But until you have developed the ability to recognize glazes and texture, and to evaluate the modeling of the figures, it is best to rely on expert guidance.

In America, according to American pottery authority John Spargo, pottery (type unknown) was made in 1641 in Salem, Massachusetts. A coarse earthenware was made by the year 1650 or earlier in the settlements of Virginia, although it is not known where or by whom the potteries were conducted. By 1657, the Dutch at New Amsterdam were making what was probably redware, but this fact is not definitely established, either. Spargo states that in writing of pre-Revolutionary potters, "it is sufficient to show that before the Revolution potteries were fairly numerous, and that in the decade preceding the fateful events of 1776, the industry had made substantial progress in the direction of improving the quality of the wares."

Up until the latter part of the eighteenth century, very little pottery was made in the United States; most was imported from England and the Far East. During the early nineteenth century, manufactories were more widespread as molded pottery became popular, and the home market was supplied commercially on a large scale with much earthenware with a variety of glazes. The American Pottery Manufacturing Company was established in Jersey City, New Jersey, in 1828, and pottery was being produced at Bennington, Vermont, around the same time and for a long period thereafter. East Liverpool, Ohio, became a pottery-making center in the 1840s—a great deal of heavy white graniteware (ironstone) was made there. Potteries were also opened in Indiana, New York, Maryland, and Pennsylvania. By the middle of the century several Southern potteries were also in operation. Majolica began to become popular around this time.

As pottery has always been of value for functional wares, and inkwells were a needed household commodity, many American potters produced them, mostly in earthenware or stoneware. The majority were made with the well and its opening central to the body, so that the empty chamber surrounding the well might accommodate and keep dry the quill or quills that could be inserted in holes placed near the well opening. At times, there was also a vent hole near the well opening, to aid in filling the well with ink.

It is important to collectors to realize that two well-known potteries operated in Bennington, Vermont. In 1793, a pottery was established there by Captain John Norton. It was owned and operated continuously for 101 years by succeeding generations of the Norton family. This pottery produced wares for common usage —jugs, crocks, and the like. Another pottery began independent operation about 1847, conducted by Christopher Webber Fenton (related by marriage to the son of the founder of the Norton pottery). A brief merger of the two firms lasted about two years, from 1845 to 1847; in 1848 Fenton went into partnership with two new men in a firm named Lyman, Fenton & Park. About 1853 this became, after several prior name changes, the United States Pottery Company.

The stands and wells made at Bennington included redware, graniteware, Rockingham, and those with flint enamel glazes. Rockingham (earthenware with a mottled brown glaze, sometimes described as having a tortoiseshell appearance) was first made in Swinton, England, at a pottery on the estate of the Marquis of Rockingham.

A rare Bennington inkstand advertised in 1841 by Julius Norton features a stoneware dog reclining on a scroll-type platform base decorated with a cobalt blue glaze. There are several Bennington inkstands of this design, and in his book *Bennington Pottery and Porcelain* Richard Carter Barret warns the collector about confusing them, and illustrates, for comparison, a similar stand made by Walley, Smith & Skinner of England.

A variety of other inkstands and inkwells were made at Bennington, including the coveted little lion's head of Rockingham. The lion's open mouth serves as the well opening. A desk set of Rockingham was made there during the nineteenth century (1854). When assembled, it looks like a steepled church, and consists of an inkwell, wafer box, sander, and penwiper. This rare item is also pictured in Mr. Barret's book.

Perhaps the most unusual inkwell made at Bennington is a graniteware one that dates from the 1850s. It depicts the various phrenology zones of the human skull. Though not often seen these

90. Sleeping boy and sleeping girl inkwells with Rockingham glaze. Both are 3¾ inches in height.

days, from time to time one turns up at an antique show. Such a specimen is a special interest to those who enjoy collecting the oddities in Americana.

For years, the so-called "Sleeping Boy" and "Sleeping Girl" inkwells, which may have been sold in pairs and which strongly resemble Bennington wares, were attributed to Bennington (see Illustration No. 90). Knowledgeable dealers, aware of this incorrect attribution, no longer sell them as Bennington items. It is now thought they may have been produced by Larkin Bros. of Newell, West Virginia.

Historical motifs were popular on inkwells in this country during the nineteenth century. One white earthenware inkstand with figures of Indians portrays the signing of the treaty of Shacka-maxon by William Penn. It was made by George S. Harker & Company of East Liverpool, Ohio.

Inkwells were also made at Rookwood Pottery, Cincinnati, Ohio, one of America's most important late-nineteenth- and early-twentieth-century potteries, which produced some of the first and finest Art Nouveau pottery made in this country. In addition to the floral motifs used on its hand-decorated wares, many showing Art Nouveau or Oriental influence, there were also pieces with incised or modeled decoration. Many were brilliantly glazed, but a mat finish was also used. All pieces, starting in 1886, were marked with the Rookwood "R-P" mark; and from the beginning many were artist-signed.

In addition to inkwells, Rookwood also made inkstands and so-called "ink trays," as well as desk or writing sets that included a dozen items. Possibly as many as a score of different types were made, and several of them incorporated a rook in the design, according to Herbert Peck, author of *The Book of Rookwood Pottery.* William F. Covill, Jr.'s *Ink Bottles and Inkwells* pictures one such traylike specimen that has the figure of a rook poised near the cuplike well. The rook-decorated pieces proved particularly popular and were continued in the firm's art pottery line for many years. Although doubtless quite a considerable number of Rook-wood wells, stands, and trays were produced over the years, they are not too often seen on the market today.

Inkwells were produced at another Ohio pottery of the late-nineteenth century, S. A. Weller of Zanesville, and no doubt numer-ous American potteries in other parts of the country also made some inkwells along with their lines of useful household items.

Large inkwells of earthenware were made for use in commercial establishments and offices, where it was necessary for a good supply of ink to be kept readily at hand. One or two of these merit a place in any collection of pottery stands and wells.

The majority of American pottery ink bottles were made of stoneware, with a variety of glazes that ranged (as did many foreign-made pottery ink bottles) from light to dark brown, and also included an off-white glaze sometimes called "white" by the manufacturer. Some bottles had dull glazes; others had shiny ones. Since ink bottles were used extensively during the nineteenth cen-tury, doubtless many American potteries produced them. Most were unmarked, and that makes attribution to a particular pottery diffi-cult. It is known, however, that pottery ink bottles were made by Boss Brothers, in Ohio, and by the Enterprise Pottery Company, New Brighton, Pennsylvania.

Some pottery inkwells and bottles had patented features. The very first patent granted for an ink bottle was given to Thaddeus Davids of New York on January 11, 1869. As was mentioned in the Introduction, he wrote a book entitled *The History of Ink.*

The marks on pottery are even more varied than the types of pottery made, and the collector will find it necessary to make fre-quent use of a book of marks. C. Jordan Thorn's book, *Handbook of*

91. In center foreground is a charming English pottery inkstand with attached wells, pottery inserts, separate covers. A colorful fruit-motif border decorates both the wells and the tray. Mark is "KALING NEW CASTLE-ON-TYNE. Made in England." The owl figural well at far left, also pottery, has a gun-metal luster finish. The head serves as the stopper. At far right is a colorful two-piece pottery well, 2¼ inches square, made during the twentieth century. The other two wells are French pottery: The square one is colorfully modernistic in design; the octagonal one is blue and has four quill holes and a hinged brass lid.

Old Pottery and Porcelain Marks, is one we have found useful. (See Bibliography.)

There is great diversity in the types of pottery inkwells and inkstands available to today's collector. They offer a broad range of designs, forms, and textures. Some have a homespun charm that is characteristic of folk arts and crafts; others, such as Wedgwood stands, have a classical beauty that makes them artistic treasures.

8

Bronze and Brass
Inkstands and Inkwells

*T*he golden glory of brass and the enduring beauty of bronze have given us inkstands and inkwells exemplifying the grandeurs and the life-styles of the past. These impressive artistic and functional objects, made from metal to serve man's aesthetic and practical desires, range from the massive to the minute. Today they are among the inkwells and inkstands easiest to acquire.

Bronze and brass are alloys of copper, man's oldest metal, for primitive man fashioned spearheads and tools from it when he found it in nugget form. Bronze is copper with the addition, chiefly, of tin; brass is copper to which zinc has been added. In color bronze ranges from brown to red-yellow; brass varies from yellow to reddish yellow. Old brass, unless buffed or lacquered, has a soft, dull tone.

Collecting objects of bronze can give one a sense of history, as civilization is said to have been "born" with the coming of the

92.   Louis XIV inkstand (circa 1750); Chinese lacquer and bronze. The underglaze blue-and-white porcelain pots were mounted in gilt bronze in France. This type of piece would originally have been used on a flat writing table, or *bureau plat*. The stand is 14 inches long. *Carnegie Institute, Museum of Art, Pittsburgh, Pa., Ailsa Mellon Bruce Collection*

Bronze Age (2500–1800 B.C.), when this alloy of copper was used prolifically for making weapons and tools. About seven thousand years ago, the Egyptians used bronze for making not only tools but even surgical instruments. The Greeks excelled in casting bronze statuary, and fifteenth-century bells of bronze at Peking, each weighing about fifty-five tons and standing fourteen feet high, testify that the Chinese made bronze objects of great size. During the Renaissance, Italy led the world in artistic bronze work. Ghiberti gave the world the wonder of his bronze doors (Michelangelo called them the Gates of Paradise) at the Baptistery of San Giovanni in Florence, and Riccio fashioned his great bronze Paschal candlestick, which is in the Basilica de Sant' Antonio in Padua.

    In the nineteenth century, there was a revival of interest in Renaissance bronze styling motivated by the fact that sand casting had replaced the laborious cire perdue (lost wax) process for making bronze statuary. Through sand casting and the use of a mechanical reducing machine, an accurate copy of a statue could be made in any size. This doubtless contributed to the popularity of decorating inkstands with bronze figures during the nineteenth century and the early part of the twentieth. A few inkstands with bronze statuettes were made in the sixteenth century by George Vischer and Peter Vischer, but such bronze pieces were rarely made then.

Bronze is very easy to work with, as it yields well to tools and when melted has the fluidity to fill molds perfectly. From long exposure to the atmosphere and repeated handling, it develops an attractive green patina. A patina can be induced to form more rapidly by artificial means, but a natural patina usually takes many years to develop. Sophisticated collectors consider a natural patina highly desirable and deplore its removal. They feel that tampering with the patina on an inkstand or inkwell destroys much of its value.

93. Bronze figural inkstand. The entire figure, 3½ inches in height, is the hinged lid to the well, which is a pressed glass insert set in a hollowed-out portion of the wooden base. The cap on the figure is also hinged. An aperture in the arm provides a resting place for the quill or pen.

94. Small and unusual Oriental bronze figural inkwell, 3 inches wide at the base and 2½ inches high. The hinged head forms the lid.

Bronze inkstands are both appealing and exciting to collect because so many of them are imaginatively figural. A court jester's head mounted on a round wooden base is found to be an inkwell when the jester's cap is tipped to reveal the glass insert. A squat Oriental figure not quite three inches tall also proves to be an inkwell. By means of a small hinge, which is the queue at the back of the finely wrought hair, the entire head can be tilted backward to disclose a bronze insert. There are endless bronze groupings of animals and humans against mythical and even allegorical landscapes that, at first glance, look like purely decorative pieces but are really inkwells. Some of these are monstrosities of overdesigning, though they do express the prevailing tastes of the late Victorian period.

95.   The pinkish bronze oval well at right has a sterling silver band on the hinged lid. This distinctively designed well is marked "AMS Sterling on Bronze Pat. August 27, 1912." There is a clear glass insert. At left is a box-type stand consisting of a wooden box decorated with Oriental bronze cutwork; inside are two unusual opaline inserts. The hinged lid bears an Oriental mountain scene with iris and flamingos. Box is 4½ inches long.

96. This magnificent green cut glass inkstand, 4 inches long and 3¼ inches wide, is enhanced by ormolu. The cover is hinged. The glass is 1¼ inches thick.

97.   Nineteenth-century French bronze inkstand, 7 inches in
height, has a marble base ranging from tan to salmon pink in
color.

When judging bronze items, it is necessary to pay attention not only to the material used, but also to the form of the object, the technique employed, and the style of decoration. If a considerable amount of money is asked for a bronze item, the prospective buyer should request some documentation of its provenance, for there has been much copying in this field and there is usually no way of telling where a piece originated.

Bronze has a superb surface quality that is warm and inviting to the touch. It can be cast with a rough surface, which absorbs light and creates the illusion of weight, or it can be given a highly polished surface that reflects light and has a mirrorlike finish. A typical example of this polished surface is a box-type oval inkwell of bronze of a faintly reddish tone with silver banding on the cover, which is shown in Illustration No. 95. It is probably of English manufacture. Bronze wells and stands with this mirrorlike finish generally follow the lines of choice silver wells and stands.

Some stands combine bronze with other materials—marble, glass, and so on. They are often classically handsome in styling. The majority are too high in price for the beginning collector and even at times, for the fairly advanced collector.

98.   French bronze inkstand depicts a humorous scene in considerable detail—the boy is attempting to climb an apple tree, but the dog has other ideas. Length is 11 inches. Circa 1880–90. *Collection of Robert Duplease*

99.   Nineteenth-century French bronze and crystal inkstand was cast by
Ferdinand Barbedienne, possibly from a design by Barye. It was recently
on display at Marble House, Newport, Rhode Island. *The Metropolitan
Museum of Art, Gift of Mrs. Henry J. Bernheim, 1947*

The French were proficient in using ormolu (gilded bronze or
brass) and made many inkstands incorporating this material. Sometimes it was used as the mount for glass inkwells. Very old French
ormolu is much prized, but the inkstands and inkwells with French
ormolu decoration available today would, in all likelihood, be of
nineteenth-century vintage. (Ormolu was also made in Germany
and England, but the French product is superior.)

Bronze inkstands decorated with statuettes executed by well-
known sculptors or illustrating exceptional period works are usually
in museums, especially those made prior to the nineteenth century.
There are still, however, many fine bronze inkstands of the nineteenth and early twentieth centuries that are worth collecting, even

though, as is usually the case, the sculptor and country of origin are unknown. Available also are a number of bronze inkwells of English styling, as well as square glass ones with bronze mountings made in France, that will satisfactorily round out a collection.

Bronze inkwells made in Vienna are highly collectible today, but Vienna bronzes are usually costly. They include a parade of highly imaginative pieces, such as a mouse sitting on a pile of crackers with another mouse sitting contentedly nearby, and are realistically painted. Generally they are genre in theme.

100.   This bronze monumentlike inkstand bears a replica of Trajan's Column in Rome. The stand is nearly 9 inches long; height is 11 inches. The black marble base is an inch thick. The spiral frieze that covers the entire surface of the column depicts Trajan's warlike exploits, and atop the column is a statue of Trajan.

101. An appealing bronze well of the late Victorian period is 5½
inches at the base and 5½ inches high. The boy's cap is the hinged lid.

102. Cast bronze inkwell, more than 4½ inches high, has deep red enamel in the recessed portions of the design. An engraved calling card, enclosed with the well when it was bought recently, reads "To Bertha, September 9, 1902" and is signed "Grandma."

103.   Enamel in pink and two shades of blue decorates this French bronze ink-stand, which is slightly more than 6 inches in diameter. Circa 1880. *Collection of Robert Duplease*

104. Choice French bronze and crystal inkwell. Overall height is 4½ inches, including the bronze mushroom-shaped hinged lid with applied filigree. The well is permanently set into a graceful bronze openwork base.

In 1897, Louis C. Tiffany, whose work is also discussed in Chapter 6, enlarged his Corona (New York) works by establishing a foundry there, and by 1899 metal (including bronze) inkstands were among the products being made. That same year, the products of the foundry exhibited at the Grafton Galleries in London included four metal inkstands—crab, dahlia, and wild carrot designs, and one with what was called "blown glass inside."

A 1902 Tiffany listing shows seventeen different "inkstands," as he generally termed them. Most are single wells with glass inlays, mosaics, or blown glass inside. But the larger ones were true inkstands and boasted a taper holder that branched gracefully out at one side—a radical departure from the traditional styles of taper holders on inkstands of earlier years.

During the first two decades of the twentieth century Tiffany

105. This tiny Vienna bronze inkwell, realistically painted, has a kind of storybook charm. The topmost cracker is the hinged lid. The smaller mouse is not quite 1½ inches in length.

produced quantities of matched desk sets. These bronze sets were usually given a green, brown, or gold finish. Some consisted of twenty or more items—calendar, rocker blotter, stamp box, tray, paper rack, blotter ends, paper knife, inkstand, lamp, letter rack, memorandum pad, reading glass, bookends, and so on—each of which was sold separately, but nine was the minimum number of items considered a set.

Tiffany's bronze inkstands were made in well over a dozen patterns: "Byzantine" (the rarest, discontinued around 1906); "Adam," "Royal Copper," "Bookmark," "Zodiac," "Venetian," "Abalone," "Graduate," "Ninth Century," "American Indian" (currently extremely popular with collectors), "Pine-needle," "Grape-vine," "Louis XVI," "Chinese," "Modeled Design," and "Nautical." A few, such as "Chinese," "Byzantine," and "Zodiac," are all bronze, ornamented with designs in high or low relief. "Adam" is decorated with green enamel; "Abalone," as its name suggests, has embedded disks of abalone shell. The "Ninth Century" inkstand is finished in gold and mounted with "jewels" of pink, green, or blue.

The first Tiffany bronzes were numbered individually and bore the trademark of Tiffany Glass and Decorating Company. In 1900 the mark "Tiffany Studios, New York" was also added. Use of the T G and D Co. marks were discontinued in 1904, and a model number

106. Tiffany "inkstands." The example at far left is in Tiffany's Etched
Metal and Glass pattern. The gold-plated metal overlay in a grapevine
motif covers amber-toned Favrile glass with a clear glass insert. (Etched
Metal and Glass items were also made with the overlay in a green finish
and in a pine-needle motif.) There is a hinged lid on this 3½-inch-square
stand. Mark is "Tiffany Studios/New York" and the model number: 845.
The original price was $15. In the center is a gold-finished Zodiac pattern
inkstand, model number 1072, also marked "Tiffany Studios/New York."
(Zodiac desk sets were available in green and brown finishes as well; the
inkstands came in three sizes, including one for a "double desk.") The
Tiffany promotional material described this pattern as "dignified and
simple in character," with "Zodiac signs carved in low relief on the
Medallions . . ." Diameter of the stand shown here is 6½ inches. The
Chinese pattern double stand at the right is model number 1763, bronze
with a brown finish. Like the other two, it is marked "Tiffany Studios/
New York" and with its model number. There were also single stands in
this pattern, and in addition to the brown finish, the pattern was made in
both green and gold finish. The Chinese pattern stand illustrated here is
5½ inches in length.

replaced the system of individual numbering. Desk sets began with Model Number 800.

Tiffany also made various individual inkstands as well as those appealing ladies' stands in a gold plate (doré) with pink enamel. Pink and blue were colors rarely used by Tiffany, and so this inkstand is doubly attractive to collectors.

Among the inkstands mentioned in a 1906 price list that is reproduced in Dr. Koch's book (*Louis C. Tiffany's Glass–Bronzes–Lamps*) is a metal butterfly stand with a poppy well; a Japanese stand; both single and triple scarab stands, and several that included the glass turtleback tiles in their construction. Even in 1906, they were not cheap—most were priced at $15 to $20, but some at two and three times that. Today, naturally, the rarer pieces sell for hundreds, even thousands of dollars, but the desk-set type of well commands a more modest sum.

As fascinating as bronze wells and stands are to collect, the warm glowing beauty of the brass specimens has its own appeal. Brass has long been a favored material for household items. During the twelfth century, brass utensils had an honored place in the

107.   Eighteenth-century brass standish, nearly 8½ inches long. The sander, inkwell, and quill holder are all unattached. The cover of the well is a bell; sander and quill holder also have separate covers. The stand is about 3½ inches wide and 7 inches high.

108. Eighteenth-century brass caster-type standish (nearly 5 inches high) has three cylindrical brass vessels—two inkwells and a quill holder—that fit into the base. All three have removable covers.

kitchen, and during the fourteenth century the production of brass wares for domestic usage reached such a height in the town of Dinant (in what is today Belgium) that the word *dinanderie* came into common use for domestic utensils of brass.

Germany, Austria, Holland, China, and many other countries have all produced brass objects in vast quantities. During the seventeenth century, England made inkstands of brass along with fine brass candlesticks and chandeliers with curved branching arms.

In the beginning, most of the brass objects used in the American Colonies had to be imported from Europe. Finally, between 1806 and 1809, the experiments of Abel Porter and his associates of Waterbury, Connecticut, resulted in the first successful American casting of brass bars. The English, who led the world in brass making at that time, were loath to share their secrets, and had

109. Eighteenth-century brass standishes: At left is a seven-part standish consisting of a base with three round recesses for holding the two cylindrical wells and the cylindrical sander. All the vessels have loose covers. The base is 8¼ inches long. The slightly longer standish at· the right has two vessels attached to the base—an inkwell and a wafer box. The urn-shaped sander is unattached. The three vessels have separate covers, but the cover on the sander, though of equal age, is not the original; it has a quill hole, as does the inkwell.

refused to export either rolls of brass or skilled brassworkers to the United States. The story is told that English brassworkers were smuggled here in barrels early in the nineteenth century. However, the demand for kettles and other household items of brass continued to grow, and soon the brass industry was flourishing in the Naugatuck River Valley, where Waterbury is located. Wagon after wagon rumbled along the rutted Connecticut roads transporting brass.

Brass kettles made by the so-called "Battery Method" were produced for the first time in this country at one of the Naugatuck River Valley towns, Wolcottville (now Torrington), about 1834. A half-century later, 200,000 tons of brass (85 percent of the nation's total output) were produced at valley mills. With so much brass available, it is small wonder that during the late nineteenth century American homes were well supplied with brass utensils and ornaments, including inkstands and inkwells.

110.   This interesting brass inkstand in the shape of an elongated clover-leaf boasts the figure of a stag and has brass frogs decorating the well lids, which slide aside to give access to the ink. Overall height is a little more than 5½ inches. Probably nineteenth century and English.

111. Metal inkwell and quill pen. *Colonial Williamsburg*

Most of the earliest brass inkstands available in any quantity to collectors today originated in England during the eighteenth century. They closely follow the lines of the silver English inkstands made contemporaneously, and have the traditional pounce pot, inkpot, and bell reposing on a footed tray-type platform stand. The cruet-type brass inkstand with two inkpots and a pounce pot, as well as the classically styled inkstand with urn-shaped vessels for pounce and ink and a similarly shaped wafer box, made about 1790, is also found from time to time at antique shows and shops, particularly at shops specializing in English antiques.

Early in the nineteenth century, in an effort to solve the problem of ink evaporation, the French devised the "pump" inkstand of brass and porcelain (mentioned briefly in an earlier chapter). The pump inkstand was made in varying styles and in different sizes, but it is not easy to buy one of them these days. Not long ago we succeeded in getting one that was located in Paris by a French dealer. This stand has a brass control knob with a plate on top bearing the inscription "ENCRIER POMP 1839 MEDAILLE D'ARGENT PARIS BOQUET BREVETE." A hollow porcelain float, which closely fits the bore of the main ink reservoir, is raised and lowered by a reverse screw when the control knob is turned. As the float is lowered, ink wells up in the tiny exterior font. When the float is raised, the ink returns to the main reservoir through a small channel at the base of the font. The cylindrically shaped porcelain well is of a lovely pale peach-beige tone (see Illustration No. 113). Not all pump inkstands are as elaborate as this one, of course, and some rest in a saucerlike tray of porcelain rather than brass.

Brass was combined with numerous materials in making inkstands and inkwells, including not only porcelain but wood, glass (often black), marble, and pottery. It was often used for the lids and to mount wells of other materials, and there are hundreds of attractive single wells and stands to be found that are combinations of brass and such other materials as marble, which are not too costly. One handsome little well that comes to mind has a square brass base and a body of honey-toned marble lidded with embossed brass. Another, a squat, cylindrically shaped brass well mounted on a black glass base, has a hinged brass lid with black glass on top.

Brass wells and stands were made, as mentioned before, in many countries, but most of them are unmarked; it is often difficult, without documentation, to establish where they were made, though

112.   Brass inkwells equipped with quills, on the conference table in the Committee Room of the Capitol, at the Colonial Williamsburg Restoration. Thomas Jefferson used quills from his own geese that he raised at Monticello. *Colonial Williamsburg*
◄

113.   This elegant French brass and porcelain pump-type inkstand is marked "Encrier Pomp Bouquet Brevete, Rue Richelieu." The peach-toned porcelain is decorated with gold. The sander has a fancy pierced screw-in cover. Matching wafer box cover is also removable. The base is 8½ inches long; the "sleigh back" pen rack behind the porcelain reservoir is 5 inches in height.

114. Brass inkstand (1880–1890) is 7½ inches in diameter and has a 3-inch cut crystal well. The eagle and dome form the cover, which is separate (not hinged). *Collection of Robert Duplease*

115. English inkstand of brass, 8¾ inches long and 6 inches wide, has two glass wells with flat, hinged brass covers and a covered brass wafer box. Circa 1870.

116. Large solid-brass well (probably Austrian) is 11½ inches in diameter. Overall height is 7 inches. The hat is hinged and serves as the cover.

117. The brass inkstand at the left with a 4-inch-square base is unmarked. The tray and the hinged lid are embossed. At center is an English Victorian-style brass inkstand with heavy embossing. The two wells are attached to the tray and have hinged covers. Overall length is 9¼ inches. No identification mark. The oval-shaped well at the right is cast metal with brass plating. Height is 2¾ inches, including the hinged cover. Unmarked; probably early twentieth century.

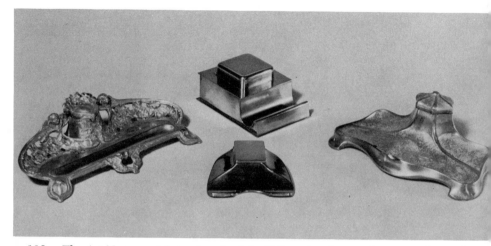

118.   The Art Nouveau inkstand at the left, 10½ inches long, is bronze with a pinkish tone. At far right is another stand in Art Nouveau style, this one of heavy cast brass. The two examples in the center are both brass and measure more than 4 inches in their longest dimension. The one in the foreground is Austrian; the one in the rear is unmarked.

119.   This heavy cast-brass inkstand of Oriental design was purchased from an English source. It is 6 inches square, including the claw feet, and 6 inches high including the Oriental figure. The decoration consists of stylized floral motifs and scroll openwork that gives it an airy grace.

styling is a clue. Sometimes the dealer will supply the names of previous owners or give the circumstances under which he acquired the well, and such information can be useful. One brass well identified by a dealer as Austrian does indeed reflect an Old World romanticism. It is the head of a cavalier with a plumed hat that lifts to disclose a glass insert; the circular brass base is mounted on a circle of wood. Then there are the brass inkpots with Oriental figures and designs, which, although unmarked, seem to have originated in the Orient and are discussed in greater detail in Chapter 3.

120.   The brass inkstand at the left, 4¼ inches square and more than 4½ inches high, including the finial on the hinged cover, is marked "W. T. & S." The cast brass stand in the center, 9¼ inches long, has two pressed glass wells with removable brass covers. Stag and hounds are depicted on the back of the stand. Mark is "B & H" (Bradley & Hubbard). At right is a square brass English stand with a well of brown-toned marble and a hinged lid. Base and height are both 4½ inches.

121. This unusual, beautifully crafted marble and brass inkstand, 13 inches in length, is marked "Fahrenheit Réaumur." Two heavy pressed glass wells fit into the stone base. Their removable covers are surmounted by finely executed scholarly items—parchment scrolls, quills, inkwells, laurel wreaths, and books with realistic-looking pages. The 6-inch figure represents René Réaumur, French scientist, born in 1683 at La Rochelle, who is best remembered for the thermometric scale that bears his name.

These inkpots were used for a black shoe-blacking kind of ink.

Beginning collectors should be encouraged by the large number of brass inkwells and inkstands available today that are not exorbitantly priced. There are some that seem to have been specifically designed for a man's desk, with mannish-looking embellishments or stylized in form; others are fairly utilitarian in appearance and may have been used in business offices, hotels, and other commercial establishments. Then there is the Plain Jane variety of small brass well, probably created to appeal to people who pre-

ferred even a simple little well to a labeled ink bottle for desk
usage. Such plain wells are usually of the Victorian or Art Nouveau
period, and well worth collecting (see Illustration No. 118), for
they will steadily increase in price if they are of good workmanship
and quality. A new collector armed with a knowledge of the appearance of old brass will not confuse these wells with the reproduced brass and glass stands and wells now frequently found in gift
shops and occasionally masquerading as antiques.

122.   The brass base of this French inkstand is covered with a mirror and
has a scroll-like pen rack at the front. The two porcelain wells with
Oriental-style decoration of flowers and birds look like flowerpots—wire
stems of ceramic flowers and metal leaves grace the hinged covers. The
predominating colors are pink, blue, and yellow. Stand is 8½ inches long
by 5 inches wide. The wells have porcelain inserts.

9

Wooden and Papier-Mâché
Inkstands and Inkwells

ood has long been a favored medium for artistic expression. Egyptians carved figureheads from wood to grace the bowsprits of their sailing vessels; Renaissance artists filled the cathedrals of Europe with rich wood carvings; English cabinetmakers used inlays of satinwood to enhance their tables and chairs; the village artisans in all countries carved everything from functional household items to gay little whistles out of wood. No doubt, the inexpensiveness and availability of wood have been the chief reason it was so widely used. Not surprisingly, it was employed extensively for the making of inkstands and inkwells.

Wooden inkwells and inkstands were probably made in all countries, but the majority of the finest ones found these days were made in England. The English seem to have been especially fond of making rectangular box-type inkstands of wood in various sizes, most of which are about ten inches long, six inches wide, and three to four inches high. They are generally of a mellow maple, oak, or

123. The walnut inkstand (English) at left with black-painted rim is 10 inches long and 6½ inches wide. The square crystal wells each measure 1½ inches. Wooden handle is also painted black. The drawer is for storage of writing paraphernalia. At right is another English wooden stand, also 10 inches long. The cut glass wells on this stand are slightly larger and have brass-hinged lids. The central handle is brass, and the drawer has a fancy brass pull. Circa 1890. In the center is a highly polished, round wooden inkwell with painted decoration in gold and a hinged lid. Diameter is 3¾ inches.

mahogany—although other woods were also used—which quite often was combined with black lacquer, brass, and even ivory. The wood in some stands is interestingly burled. Usually, these stands hold two inkwells of cut or pressed glass with matching hinged glass lids—or metal (often brass) ones. The wells fit snugly beside a centrally located wood or brass handle that arches up from the stand. A channel for pens runs across the front of the stand, just above one or two drawers for holding other writing equipment.

When buying such stands, make sure the glass vessels match each other and also match the style of the stand. The box itself should be examined carefully to see if it is in good condition and not warped. Sometimes new glass vessels have replaced the missing old ones in old wooden stands. This naturally detracts from the value of a stand, although there are antique dealers who urge customers to buy stands without wells or with replaced wells, assuring them that appropriate old glass wells are not hard to find. We have not found it a simple matter to find two wells of matching style that will properly fit a particular old stand. However, if a stand is priced low and you want to risk a small sum, there is always the chance that you may find wells to fit it.

The English were also fond of making circular and oval wooden inkstands. Some oval ones are as large as twelve by nine inches, and have an inch-thick base, perhaps mounted on pad feet. On one, a hexagonal compartment is carved out toward the back of the oval to hold the heavy four-inch hexagonal well of pressed glass, which has a sunburst motif on the bottom. The glass lid is dome-shaped and brass-hinged. A crescent, or bow-shaped, pen tray is hollowed out in the front of this stand (see Illustration No. 124).

No doubt many woodcarvers could not resist the temptation to express their talent by making figural wells of wood. An unusual one of this type is in the shape of a poodle's head, carved from ebony. The dog's mouth is open just wide enough to store a pen, ready for instant use.

124. This 12-inch oval stand has brass and ivory cutouts secured to the wood base by brass studs of various shapes and designs. Pen tray is painted black. The pressed glass well, 4½ inches in diameter, has a brass-hinged lid.

125. Head of a poodle, carved from wood and painted black, is nearly 4½ inches long. It has realistic glass eyes; the cobalt blue glass insert is attributed to Sandwich. The mouth is specially designed to hold the wood-handled pen.

Probably because the majority of them could be made and sold inexpensively, souvenir wooden inkwells and inkstands were great favorites. They ranged from large to fairly small ones. A small souvenir stand (four inches in diameter) made in France has a tiered circular base of pine on which a few violets are painted. A tiny pressed glass well with a matching wooden lid fits snugly into this wooden base, which was inscribed with the name of the place where the stand was sold.

Of a more impressive nature are the wooden trophy inkstands that were awarded for sporting events and other contests in England. They include the box type, platform type, and those with motifs representative of the particular sport for which they were awarded. A plaque was usually attached to the stand, appropriately inscribed and bearing the champion's name.

Many English wooden inkstands and inkwells are not marked with a maker's name. This makes it necessary to become familiar with the styles (box, platform tray, and so forth) in which they

126. A trophy inkwell more than 12 inches wide has a wooden base painted black and three wooden pad feet. The cut crystal octagonal well, 3 inches in diameter, has a brassbound hinged lid. Harness-type decoration is also brass, and a brass shield secured to the stand directly in front of the well reads "Kenelm Edward Digby/Hurdle Race/The Grove/Harrow/March 31, 1855."

127. Wooden Silliman inkwell used in Abraham Lincoln's law office. *Illinois State Historical Library*

were made. It is worthwhile learning as much as possible about them, for the mellow old woods glow handsomely when polished, and add contrasting texture to a collection.

In America, the Silliman patented pine inkwells of the mid-nineteenth century are probably the best-known wooden wells. They were made primarily by S. Silliman & Company of Chester, Connecticut, and were sold as "inkstands." Among the types made were the "Counting House Inkstand" (circular with curved sides and quill holes), which was made—according to a Silliman advertisement that appeared in the mid-1800s—in sizes ranging from approximately three to about six inches in diameter. Their "School Inkstand" came in five sizes, from about two inches to approximately three inches in diameter. Each "stand" contained a small glass bottle for ink (the bottle was inserted through a hole in the bottom of the stand). The bottle base was fitted with a spring, and when a plug was pressed into the hole, the bottle was held firmly in place. After the well was used, the screw cap was placed in position, the bottle depressed and firmly held against a seal, which was part of the inside of the cap. An air chamber surrounding the bottle was designed to prevent the ink from freezing. As a further safeguard, Silliman & Company advised keeping the ink bottle corked, and for this purpose a cork was attached by a cord to the body of the "inkstand." The "School Inkstand" was sold with or without gold decoration. The "Counting House Inkstand" had grained sides and a painted black top.

128. Kidney-shaped French inkstand of wood, 6¾ inches long and almost 2 inches thick, is very well made. In addition to the brass well and sander, there are a brass candleholder, a quill holder, and a container for sealing wax. Probably early nineteenth century.

The Silliman company labeled their wells, and if the paper labels are missing, the well does not command as high a price. Similar wells were made by other companies, notably by James L. Chappell of Buffalo, New York, and the Chappell wells also had paper labels.

Rosewood inkwells with screw caps inlaid with a disk of mother-of-pearl look much like little pepper mills. They, along with wells in the form of crudely carved little animals, walnuts, apples, and heads, are seen from time to time. Doubtless the latter were the work of talented amateurs who whiled away leisure hours making them for friends and relatives in the days when Christmas gifts were likely to be handmade. Most are not of great value, but they do demonstrate the ingenuity of Americans in those years, who "made do" with available wood and paint. They have a kind of grass-roots appeal.

Wooden inkstands and wells represent the kind of durable and inexpensive articles once sought for everyday usage. They are still worth preserving today.

129.   English wooden inkstands. The glass well in the walnut stand at left has a star cut in the base and in the brass-hinged lid. (Stand is 12 inches wide; well, 3 inches in diameter.) The well fits into a round wooden frame; the front of the stand serves as a pen tray. The Georgian mahogany stand at right is bound with brass on all three levels. The two crystal wells have mushroom-shaped hinged lids. The carved recess for pens is 8½ inches in length. Circa 1820.

Papier-Mâché Inkstands and Inkwells

Papier-mâché captivated the hearts of Victorians. Their parlors were filled with small boxes, albums, and sundry trinkets made of it, and their writing tables and desks were often adorned with papier-mâché writing portfolios, pencil boxes, and inkstands or inkwells. It is easy to understand why the Victorians, who were so fond of embellishment, were charmed by papier-mâché. In keeping with the taste of the times, it was decorated with chinoiserie, landscapes, exotic birds, and bouquets of flowers and often lavishly inlaid with slivers of shiny mother-of-pearl and further enhanced with gold leaf.

The art of making papier-mâché (translated from the French, it means "chewed paper") was practiced centuries ago by the Chinese, Persians, and Indians, but it was given renewed prominence in Europe by Robert and Étienne Martin of Germany. These two brothers came to Paris in the 1740s to work under royal patronage. They developed a kind of transparent lac varnish called *vernis Martin*, which they applied over paintings of scenes, fruit, flowers, and other subjects against backgrounds of emerald green, blue, and flecked gold that appeared on papier-mâché furnishings. The beauty of *vernis Martin* finish made articles bearing it prized by the French. To own a *vernis Martin* snuffbox was to possess an eighteenth-century French prestige symbol; the choicest of such snuffboxes were seen in court circles all over Europe.

Just prior to the Martin brothers' development of this art, a German living in Berlin named Johann Heinrich Stobwasser (about 1722) had developed another type of papier-mâché. Although his work was not as exquisite as the Martins', it did employ fine paintings in color.

The secret of the Martin brothers' formula for *vernis Martin* died with them, but in 1772, while trying to find a substitute for the carvings used on mantels, doors, coach panels, and such, Henry Clay, an English japanner, patented a type of papier-mâché prepared from strong sheets of paper pasted together. In the strict sense of the word, his product was a form of, but not a true, papier-mâché, which is made of mashed paper mixed with glue, chalk, and fine sand, then pressed into a mold, dried in an oven, and finally japanned. (Japanning consists of varnishing and decorating in the Japanese manner.)

The making of such papier-mâché articles as trays and furniture spread from Birmingham, where Henry Clay manufactured them, to Wolverhampton. From 1816 to 1864, the firm of Jennens and Bettridge (Birmingham) became leaders in the field, making numerous good-quality articles of papier-mâché. Clay had called his products Paper Ware, but because Jennens and Bettridge felt this name was a drawback, they sold their wares under the name of papier-mâché, for which they had perfected their own formula. This called for thick porous paper, which they soaked in a mixture of flour, glue, and water before laying three or four sheets of it in a metal mold. After the paper had been dried for twelve hours at a temperature of 90 to 100 degrees Fahrenheit, the entire process was repeated until the desired thickness was attained—usually ¼ inch, which required about ten layers. Jennens and Bettridge made a variety of articles of their papier-mâché, including inkstands. One is pictured in Shirley Spaulding DeVoe's book, *English Papier-Mâché of the Georgian and Victorian Periods.*

One of the choice papier-mâché items made in England was the popular lap desk, which, beneath a slanted lid, usually contained a velvet-topped writing board that covered a compartment for stationery. The front of the box had a slot for pens, a compartment for an ink vessel (usually glass with a separate cover of metal), and a small square box to hold sealing wafers. Generally the lap desk was fitted with a small white-metal or silver lock and key. The decoration of gold, paint, and pearl shell was generally concentrated on the lid of the desk.

Similar portable desks were produced by several makers, including Ebenezer Sheldon. Thomas Lane of Birmingham and London gave his lap desks—or "escritoires," as he called them—the difference of "pearl glass" panels set into the lid, and he held a patent on this feature.

Another favored item sold in England was a papier-mâché writing table. There was great demand for items like these and for other papier-mâché articles during the Victorian period—in fact, some homes had entire ceilings covered with papier-mâché.

In dating an inkstand or inkwell of papier-mâché, a knowledge of the types of decorations used during various periods can be of some assistance. Bronze decoration was the first type; it was used about 1812 in conjunction with powdered metals and alloys applied with swabs of various sizes. Later, bronze was applied to represent sunlight streaming through cathedral windows or on historic sites—Westminster Abbey, the Tower of London, and Warwick Castle were extremely popular subjects. Gold leaf and gold powder, however, were the most commonly used papier-mâché decoration. Mother-of-pearl inlay came into vogue about 1825; Jennens and Bettridge used green and pink shell inlay on their papier-mâché, arranged so that one of the colors predominated. Oil painting was used from the 1830s.

Reuben Thomas Neale painted a famous dog, Friend (honored because he saved his master from drowning), on an inkstand by McCallum and Hudson, the firm that eventually succeeded Jennens and Bettridge. Friend was a popular subject for papier-mâché furnishings and Staffordshire figures.

As is the case with pottery and porcelain, the work of certain artists who decorated papier-mâché (during the early years of the Victorian period) was avidly sought. George Neville was most noted for his painting of flowers on black, whereas William Bourne was famous for his painted verbenas; David Sargent made the fern pattern, usually in brilliant green, an outstanding papier-mâché motif.

Toward the latter part of the nineteenth century, so much inferior and even gaudy work in papier-mâché was produced that the medium fell from popular favor. Today interest has been revived and there are many collectors. Fortunately, there are still excellent papier-mâché inkstands and inkwells available, although they have risen in price within the past few years as the demand increased.

In America, papier-mâché was made in a number of towns, but there was never a major center of production. Good American papier-mâché (American papier-mâché never equaled the English ware in quality) was made at Litchfield, Connecticut, by the Litchfield Manufacturing Company, founded about 1849. Japanners from England directed the work at the Litchfield establishment and instructed local women in the art of japanning and painting. It is of interest to realize that these workers, when experienced, were paid a high wage—six to ten dollars a day. The Litchfield papier-mâché was made in limited quantities, and to our knowledge no records indicate that inkstands were made there.

130. Inkstand of papier-mâché, about 10 inches long and 6 inches wide, is decorated with gold geometric scrolls, designs in blue, maroon, and white enamel, and mother-of-pearl inlay (on the border). The clear cut-glass wells, 1⅜ inches square, have uncovered Sheffield tops, each with an aperture for a pen. There is an ivory finial on the wafer box. At the right is a papier-mâché writing box almost 10½ inches long. In the fore-ground, in front of this box, is a typical clear glass well with screw top of pewter, of the sort customarily found in these boxes. In the center fore-ground is a round, scalloped papier-mâché saucer, 6 inches in diameter. The attached well has a hinged lid, and both well and lid have gold and white japanning.

Paper-mâché was also made in Torrington, about five miles from Litchfield, where Pearl Street derived its name from the fact that it was in the vicinity of the Wadhams Manufacturing Company (a mid-nineteenth-century papier-mâché shop), which always had a great deal of discarded scrap mother-of-pearl strewn about. This company produced lap desks ornamented with gold leaf, bronze powders, paint, and pearl shell.

A maker of "Modern & Antique" (baroque) ornaments, Bowler, Tileston & Company of Boston advertised numerous papier-mâché items of their own manufacture in 1853—oval frames, mirrors, ladies' workboxes. Inkstands, although not specifically mentioned, were probably also produced by this firm, which made quantities of papier-mâché articles for many years. The advertisement boasted of the qualities of the papier-mâché manufactured at this plant in Boston, stating "it weighs only about one quarter as much as plaster, and is incomparably more durable. It has already, in the city of Boston, been put as carved work upon rosewood and black Walnut Furniture." The advertisement went on to say that the papier-mâché was made "in imitation of various kinds of wood, without paint and colored throughout by a process discovered by Messrs. Bowler and Tileston, so that a fracture will not deface it."

Most of the papier-mâché inkwells and inkstands seen in antique shops and shows these days were made in England. Many were recently brought to this country by antique dealers who regularly go abroad to buy stock. Those who specialize in English antiques are excellent sources for papier-mâché inkstands and wells.

In his book *Victorian, the Cinderella of Antiques,* Carl W. Drepperd pictures an elaborate papier-mâché inkstand with mirror by Matifat of Paris, 1850. The figures at the top of the stand support an oval surmounting two columns that rise from the intricately designed base. When a watch was placed in the oval, the stand became a clock as well and served a dual purpose.

Inkstands of this material are often of the rectangular platform type resting on pad feet. Geometric decorations are not considered as desirable as other kinds. The type of goldleaf ornamentation and the workmanship are prime factors in evaluating papier-mâché. It should be borne in mind, too, that gold paint was never used for decoration on a valuable piece of papier-mâché.

Papier-mâché inkwells are sometimes seen cemented to saucer-like trays, which measure about five or six inches in diameter. At times the inkpot, which is usually lidded, and the tray are japanned. Some knowledge of japanning is useful for evaluating the quality of the workmanship and the inkwell itself. However, there are authorities who warn that the type of japanning used for papier-mâché should not be confused with the Oriental work; that which is used on papier-mâché, they say, is merely a fine grade of painting.

In buying papier-mâché inkwells and inkstands, there are several other points to weigh and check. The finish should be shiny and not rough to the touch; the pearl inlay should be level with the surface (accomplished by repeated varnishing of the article); the pieces of pearl in the best work are arranged to reflect the same color primarily; and, as mentioned previously, the painting on a stand should be of good execution and aesthetically appealing.

Papier-mâché was originally considered a tough, hard product, but a good deal of it has deteriorated through the years. Yet enough sound specimens remain, mostly unmarked and by the less famous makers, so that collecting papier-mâché inkstands and inkwells can be both a successful and a satisfying hobby.

10

Miscellaneous Inkstands and Inkwells

*T*here are a number of inkstands and inkwells that do not fall within the specific chapter classifications of this book, but they deserve mention. Among them are wells and stands of pewter, stone, iron, lead, nickel silver, horn, quartz, and shell, as well as a number of novelties and those of Art Deco style.

Pewter

In the American Colonies, pewter was considered almost indispensable. It served many needs—everything from buttons and buckles to porringers and teapots was made of it—and for many years it was referred to as "poor man's silver." Pewter is an alloy of mostly tin with various amounts of copper, antimony, bismuth, and (at times) lead. The greater the amount of lead, the softer and heavier the pewter.

By the eighteenth century pewter articles were used in most homes, although the rich clung to the prestigious silver. Unfortunately, few eighteenth-century pewter pieces have survived. Being soft, they were easily damaged. Pewter also corrodes, and it melts when exposed to direct heat. Many of the damaged early pieces were melted down for reuse, to make new articles, but later pieces also sometimes deteriorated or became bent or so badly dented that they were discarded. Hence, really old pewter items are not plentiful.

In England in about the middle of the eighteenth century, pewter was followed by britannia, an excellent grade of pewter so named to give it greater sales appeal. This was first produced in America about 1810, but no evidence exists of the first maker. We know, however, that britannia was made by Ashbil Griswold of Meriden, Connecticut, in the early 1800s, and in 1814 by Israel Trask and Eben Smith of Beverly, Massachusetts. One of the best-known names in the story of American pewter and britannia is "Boardman"—several Boardmans were famed pewterers. Almost all pewter made in America after 1825 was britannia, and many of the pieces have a "mass-produced" look. But britannia is now avidly collected, although it was once frowned upon by serious collectors.

Most of the pewter inkwells commonly seen are of nineteenth-century vintage, circular in form and of various sizes. They are sometimes called "countinghouse" inkwells (Boardman & Hart of New York sold them to countinghouses). There are usually a couple of quill rests on the surface, near the well. This form of well originated in the sixteenth century, but was made in ensuing centuries. The countinghouse well was also issued by the Scottish government for use in its offices. The bottom of the Scottish well is marked with an impressed crown, with the letter "S" at the left and an "O" on the other side. It was probably made in England.

In the seventeenth century, a flat dishlike tray was attached to the circular well, a style also made in later years. Some of these pewter specimens have hinged lids. Quite a few such wells are found today at antique shows, especially among displays featuring oddments of Americana.

A box-type pewter inkstand was also made, similar to those of silver popularly used in England during the eighteenth century.

131. This pewter inkpot with five quill holes is displayed today on Thomas Jefferson's revolving desk at Monticello. Diameter of the base, 7¼ inches; height of the pot, 2¼ inches. *Thomas Jefferson Memorial Foundation*

These pewter stands—or writing boxes, as they are sometimes called—often have two compartments and a double lid with a hinge running down its length. The compartment located at the front of the stand usually contains vessels for ink, pounce, and wafers; the other is used for quills.

Pewter was made by the Swiss, Dutch, Chinese, French, and Germans, as well as by the English and Americans. Identification is difficult, for the touchmarks or makers' marks require study. Collectors who intend to specialize in pewter wells should equip themselves with a good book on pewter marks, such as *Pewter in America: Its Makers and Their Marks* by Ledlie Irwin Laughlin. The collector who intends to buy only one or two pewter wells as representative examples, however, can rely on the advice of a reliable dealer who specializes in pewter.

132. At left are two pewter inkwells of the countinghouse type. The larger one, 3¼ inches in diameter and 2¼ inches high, is marked with a crown, with a letter S on the left and an O on the right. The smaller one is unmarked. At far right is an all-horn inkwell 2 inches square. The finely polished body is deep brown with reddish highlights. The button-like cover is removable. (Another kind of horn inkwell was made with a screw cap inlaid with a mother-of-pearl disk, and a tapered cylindrical body about 1½ inches in both diameter and height.) Shown here, second from right, is a gutta-percha inkwell, dark brown in color and 2 inches in height.

Pewter was used for the covers of many glass inkwells. At times, it is also seen encasing a glass well, no doubt to protect it from breakage.

Stone

The crudely formed stone inkwells ordinarily sold by dealers who specialize in early American or the more primitive antiques are not found too often these days. Sometimes these have drilled quill holes.

Some wells were made of marble, but most were made of soap-stone, which was readily obtainable in the New England states in earlier times. During the last few years, interest in objects made of soapstone has quickened, and this, of course, has caused many of the available soapstone wells to be snapped up by collectors.

There is nothing particularly good-looking about most stone wells, but because they were usually made by amateurs, they illustrate a type of folk art. Stone wells of earlier centuries are, of course, museum pieces.

Highly refined inkstands and inkwells made of various kinds of stone were produced during the late nineteenth and early twentieth centuries. Among the stones then used were alabaster, marble, and so on; sometimes the stone was combined with another material, such as brass.

Iron

Much of the iron that provided essential wares for the American colonists came to this country from England in bar form; manufactured iron items were also imported. But, in 1644, an ironworks was established at Saugus, Massachusetts, and it was followed by a succession of other iron foundries. In America iron was generally converted into practical articles by the village blacksmith, who was

133. Honey-toned alabaster inkstand, approximately 11 inches long, has attached wells with hinged lids. Twentieth century.

134.   Cast-metal inkstands. At left is a Victorian-style stand with bronze finish, 8¾ inches long, with a matching but separate embossed cover on the glass well, which fits down into stand. The fraternal-type stand at center also has a bronze finish. The antlers of the elk form the pen rack. The 2½-inch-square pressed glass well in Swirl pattern has a separate cast-metal lid in the same pattern. Mark is "Bradley & Hubbard." At far right is an unusual embossed black cast-iron stand, 5 inches long. Two drawers pull out for access to two identically shaped well inserts, one of milk glass and the other of clear glass.

as adept at making andirons and other useful objects as he was at shoeing horses. By 1840, the introduction of cast iron made more refined work possible, and it was no longer necessary to import such iron items as hinges and locks.

The small decorative articles of cast iron that were literally poured forth by American firms from 1860 through the 1880s included countless inkstands and inkwells. Quantities of cast-iron "hotel inkstands" (Illustration No. 73) were made to supply the numerous inns and hotels that sprang into existence as traveling conditions improved. The iron frames that support the glass ink vessels on these were usually painted black, and the back of the frame ordinarily rose high enough above the back of the stand to form a pen rack. The pressed glass wells were usually square and had either hinged or loose iron lids, which matched the stand in design.

Revolving inkstands with glass fonts are often referred to today as snail inkstands because the fonts resemble snail shells. These stands were usually made with cast-iron frames, which were given various finishes, including gold-bronzed, black and gold, all gold, brown, and even nickel and blue. The fonts might be of either clear or colored glass—cobalt, blue, green, or milk white. Revolving inkstands generally had just one or two fonts; three-font stands were made, though they are scarce today.

Cast iron was used for the frame of one type of inkstand with a swinging cap that was patented about 1879. In fact, it was used for hundreds of inkstands and inkwells in a wide variety of shapes and sizes, all modestly priced. Many of them were used in offices, for they were durable and, of course, inexpensive. A large number of the glass single wells with cast-iron lids seen today were originally part of a single or double cast-iron inkstand.

Some of these wells and stands are marked with makers' names; others are not so marked and may have been imported. Several carry patent imprints, which aid in establishing their age.

Lead, White Metal, and Various Lead-Containing Alloys

Lead was used much more for the long parade of toy soldiers that have amused children down through the years than it was for inkwells and inkstands. An almost square, crude type of lead inkwell cast in a mold, with or without quill holes and strongly resembling the soapstone wells, was made during the late eighteenth and into the nineteenth century in this country, probably in the East, it is believed. (Lately we have seen reproductions of this type of well.) A simple round lead well was also cast in a mold and, like the squarish ones, doubtless was produced by a number of the small firms that also cast pewter and brass items. A few lead wells were so crude that it can only be concluded they were made by hand. Initials appear on some lead inkwells; most have no marking at all, and consequently cannot be attributed to any maker for they have no distinguishing features.

A considerable number of inexpensive inkstands and inkwells of certain lead-containing alloys and of white-metal alloys (nickel

135. Group of figural inkwells, mostly of lead alloys. The tallest, the sitting bear, is 4¾ inches high. In the bottom row, the Oriental woman, the donkey beside a tree-trunk well, and the bird-on-chimney well are colorfully painted. The dog well in this row is also painted. The signed Pairpoint stand with a pug dog and the sitting bear wells are white metal. The hinged head of the bear is the lid. The carp well has a bronze-like finish. The head of the fish lifts for access to the well.

silver, for one) are available today. During the late nineteenth and early twentieth century, such metals were used for charming little painted figural wells and for inkstands—some of fairly elaborate late Victorian design. Those of nickel silver generally followed the lines of the Victorian silver or brass inkstands.

The figural wells (Illustration No. 135) include such delightful little genre pieces as a gaily painted bird sitting on a red chimney on a rooftop. Another has a little donkey tied to a tree stump, which is actually the ink container. A sitting bear with a head that lifts to reveal a well insert was also a favorite.

Lead alloy wells of a highly refined nature would seem, judging from their shape and style, to have emanated from foreign countries. One stand of this type, minutely detailed, is shaped like a gondola. The gondolier holds a brass oar, and the exterior of the

136. This highly refined and minutely detailed gondola well is made of a lead alloy. The gondolier holds a brass oar. The "cabin" lifts to reveal two wells. This piece is 17 inches long; at the widest point it measures 2½ inches. Similar boats were made in other sizes.

"cabin" lifts to reveal a double well with copper inserts. Its surface is embossed (Illustration No. 136).

Most of these stands and inkwells are unmarked, and so without documentation it is difficult to ascertain just where they were made. As might be expected, a number of them were imported from other countries, including Germany. They usually prove to be prime conversation pieces.

Horn

In America during the early days, the horns of oxen were used for inkwells because horn is very light and strong, bounces when dropped, and even floats. Its durability made it an acceptable material for inkwells in those days of rugged living when people had to make use of the materials at hand.

Very few horn inkwells are seen these days, and it may take the collector a considerable amount of time and effort to find one. Most examples are relatively small in size, whether round or square. Some horn wells appear to have been machine-made (Illustration No. 132). Those we have seen have generally been unmarked, but an occasional one has initials on the base.

Shell

During the mid-nineteenth century, the Victorians developed a great fondness for the delicate beauty of shell, or mother-of-pearl, decoration. It appeared for a time on tea caddies, card cases, and knife handles, as well as on hundreds of other items, including inkstands and inkwells (as was mentioned in an earlier chapter). Eventually shell decoration was used to cover the entire surface of such objects as inkstands.

The portion of the shell obtained for decoration was the innermost lining, generally of the shell of the pearl oyster. The beautiful Sulu oyster shell was also much sought for use as decoration. Abalone shell was used too. The pieces of shell were shaped on a horizontal grinding wheel. None of these shell wells were, to our knowledge, marked.

137.   An unusual inkwell cut from a large, delicately colored shell appears at left. Although the piece is shaped like a fish, it mainly follows the natural contours of the shell. It is decorated with cuttings resembling scrimshaw work, and has a well with a hinged lid secreted at the top of the fish's head. Undoubtedly handmade, this is an excellent example of the shell inkwells created by imaginative artisans. At center rear is a beautifully crafted boat-shaped inkstand entirely covered with colorful abalone. The glass well rests in a velvet-lined recess and has a hinged, silver-plated abalone lid. Approximately 7 inches long. The prized tiger-eye inkwell, more than 1½ inches in diameter, has a silver-hinged lid. At far right is an example of the much-sought-after cloisonné inkwell, 2¼ inches square, with separate cover. There is a glass insert.

Quartz and Gemstones

Inkwells and stands constantly turn up that graphically illustrate the craftsman's desire to create a "jewel" or a unique or especially different item. Such a well is one of rose quartz with intricate carving that is in a private collection. This exquisitely fashioned little well, about 3 inches in diameter and 3½ inches high, was no doubt made to please a wealthy client. Wells of this type were also made of onyx, jade, and even tiger eye (see Illustration No. 137). Usually these gemlike wells are of superior craftmanship and design and command prices beyond the budget of the new collector who must limit his expenditures or even, at times, of any but the most sophisticated collectors. If one can afford such a well, it is worth the investment.

Cloisonné

The cloisonné inkwells that appear every now and then in an antique shop or show deserve consideration. Cloisonné is a form of enameling in which the surface decoration consists of enamel inset in bent-wire compartments (cloisons) secured to a metal base. Metal wires or ribbons are fastened to the metal base (usually copper) to form the decorative design or pattern. Then the various compartments are repeatedly filled with enamels of the colors required by the design, and fired until they melt and fuse. Finally, the surface of the piece is polished.

Both China and Japan have long produced cloisonné pieces of fine quality, and Oriental cloisonnés frequently appear on the market today. As far as cloisonné inkwells are concerned, the few that we have seen are unmarked. Generally, they are simple in form but attractive and colorful. For an example of such a well, see Illustration No. 137.

Art Deco

The Art Nouveau era was followed by what is today called Art Deco style, which—in sharp contrast to the free-flowing lines of Art Nouveau—was characterized by angles, squares, sunbursts, pyramids, and Egyptian motifs. Art Deco wells and stands include many made of black glass, hammered copper or brass, or brightly colored, modernistically designed pottery. Chrome decoration was common on wells and stands in this style.

The Art Deco style was first highlighted at L'Exposition Internationale des Arts Décoratifs et Industriels in Paris in 1925. The name "Art Deco" derives from the French term Arts Décoratifs. In 1966 at a Paris commemorative exhibition, the shortened form "Art Déco" was used, and during that same year the term appeared without the accent in the London *Times*. It has been said that Art

Deco is not so much a single style as a complex of styles and tastes, which ended the snobbish distinction that had existed between art and industry for so many years.

Young people today seem particularly drawn to Art Deco articles, which are nostalgic reminders of the 1920s and early 1930s—the age of jazz and F. Scott Fitzgerald.

Novelties

Novelty wells and stands are a highly diverse category. In the other chapters of this book, we have already mentioned numerous wells that can be considered as novelties, but a few more should have specific mention. For example, this category includes the gaudy, inexpensively made, and often poorly designed ones that were popularly bought around the turn of the century as vacation

138. Collectible souvenir specialties: The sterling silver street-cleaner's cart at left is accurate in every detail. Its four wheels move on axles, and it has a copper liner. Doubtless it once had a sterling silver shovel that served as a pen (with the nib attached to the handle). The glass insert for ink is blown. Purchased at Martha's Vineyard, this piece is marked "Mappin & Webb." The wooden stand in the center foreground bears a pressed glass well with separate wooden cap. It is decorated with hand-painted violets and marked "St. Anne de Beaupré." Behind this wooden stand is an Oriental brass writing case of a very old type. At far right, the round wooden inkwell, 2 inches in diameter, has a brass insert and a hinged silver cover. The silver shield on the side reads "Souvenir of Guam."

souvenirs. In spite of their inferior quality, many of these have been snapped up by collectors of souvenirs. We have seen them of such materials as wood and glass, crudely made, brightly painted with flowers, and bearing the name of a city or some popular vacation resort. Not all these souvenirs, however, were of inferior crafting; some were attractive and well made, to appeal to the more sophisticated (see Illustration No. 138), and these make desirable acquisitions.

Inkstands and inkwells of various materials, including glass and metal, that were made for sale at fairs and expositions are sought today, not only by inkwell collectors but by those who concentrate on acquiring souvenirs of this type. An inkwell was issued representing the well-known Memorial Hall, one of the buildings at the Philadelphia Centennial Exposition of 1876. This well of clear crystal is about seven inches by four inches in size. The dome of the building serves as the lid for the inkpot beneath it. On the underside of the well base is the inscription: "Charles Yockel Estab. 1855, 235 Broad St. Phila. Pa. U.S.A. Glass Mould Maker 1876." Many cut glass items were displayed and sold at this exposition, and tremendous interest was aroused in cut glass. Doubtless inkwells were among the many small and easily portable cut-glass items available for purchase. Probably most of these were not marked as souvenirs, and so through the years they have lost their identity as Exposition mementos.

Inkwells and stands were also made from war souvenirs—shells and rifle parts. Great care and much attention to detail, as well as no small amount of ingenuity, often went into the creation of these wells, and they are eagerly sought by collectors of war memorabilia.

There are also wells and stands that were made specifically for the members of various fraternal organizations (Masons, Elks, and so on). (See Illustration No. 139.) These were produced in a wide variety of materials and shapes and were often well constructed. They too are considered collectible today. We have found those issued for the Elks easier to acquire, but from time to time also come upon those bearing the Masonic emblem. A few years ago, a dealer who owned a clear glass inkstand with a Masonic emblem told us that one similar to his was, at that time, on a desk at Mount Vernon. During the first years of the twentieth century, club and lodge activities were important "social" events in a community, and

139.   Fraternal inkstand. This gilded inkstand was the proud possession
of the authors' father, Charles H. Rivera, a member of the local Elks
Lodge. As children they recall seeing it on the family desk, and it is as
much a part of their childhood memories as his pearl-handled penknife
with the B.P.O.E. insignia. The stand is unmarked, but probably was
made by Bradley & Hubbard.

so it is easy to believe that fraternal association inkstands and inkwells were regarded as distinctive gifts or presentation pieces.

In our judgment, the "seated camel" metal inkwells are un-attractive novelty pieces—we have always passed up the opportunity to buy one. We feel the same way about the brightly painted, molded composition wells in the form of animal heads—sometimes bears or lions. The head usually has a hinged mouth; when opened, it reveals horrid large teeth and a brilliant tongue behind which an inkwell is concealed.

Novelty wells and stands are not always inexpensively priced these days. There are collectors who avidly seek souvenirs and oddities, and are willing to pay high prices for them.

11

Writing Accessories
and Implements

s a collection of inkwells, inkstands, and ink
bottles is being assembled or upgraded, the collector finds himself becoming more and more interested in other
writing accessories and the various implements—pens of all sorts,
inks, sanders, seals, glue pots, and the like.

Pens

Man has used everything from his fingers to rushes, reeds,
quill pens, metal nibs, and our present-day ball-point and fiber
pens to convey his thoughts and record his activities since that long-
ago time when he put pictures and symbols on the walls of caves. It
is impossible to overemphasize the importance of the art of writing,
for to it we owe most of our knowledge of the past.

Primitive man used his fingers to draw in the dirt or sand. Then

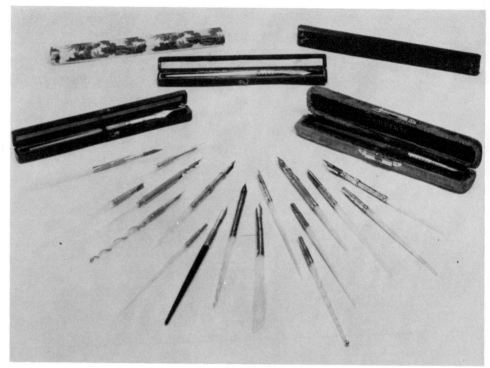

140. The number of pen collectors is growing. The pens illustrated here, however, represent only a small sampling of the variety available. Also highly collectible are presentation boxes with the original pens in them. They were made of various materials. Of the boxes shown, one is covered with red plush; the others are covered with leather in red, blue, or black. The white silk lining in the cover of one of these boxes is inscribed "Alice's Birthday, July 7, 1873." The box contains a slender gold-filled and pearl penholder with its gold-filled nib gleaming against the purple velvet lining of the bottom of the box. The poinsettia- and holly-patterned box (*top left*) encloses a Christmas-gift pen. As mentioned in the text, the pen was preceded by the quill—and early in the nineteenth century the ends of some quills were gilded to make them last longer. In 1819 James Lewes invented an ink-flow pen that was controlled by a lever. This was followed by various other types of pens. Charles Goodyear manufactured a vulcanized rubber pen in 1853; Lewis Waterman made pens in 1884.

he turned to a pointed stone or the charred end of a stick so that he might put his markings on the walls of his home, which was probably a cave. The Sumerians invented cuneiform characters and symbols. They chiseled them into stone and, in later years, onto boxwood tablets covered with wax, using a stylus of metal, bone, or ivory, sharp at one end and blunt at the other (for "erasures"). This form of writing was practiced by a number of ancient peoples, including the Babylonians, Assyrians, Armenians, and Persians, and was used until after the birth of Christ. Although the stylus is considered the oldest writing implement, it is marsh reed that is the true precursor of the modern pen. Before 4000 B.C., the Egyptians used reeds and rushes; the Chinese wrote with a brush pen of camel or rat hair for at least a full millennium before the coming of Christ. The early Romans and Greeks employed both the stylus and the sharpened reed; it is believed that Jerome, in the fourth century, used such a pen when he translated the Greek and Hebrew scriptures into the Latin Vulgate.

Quill pens came into use as early as the seventh century, possibly earlier, and remained the writing tool of the civilized Western world for over a thousand years. They were commonly made of the tail feathers of geese, the best quality quills being obtained from Russia and Holland. A quill pen was not very durable—usually it had to be replaced in a few days, though it is said that Sir Walter Scott wrote an entire novel with one goose quill that came from the Hudson Bay area.

The word "pen" came to us from the Latin word *penna* (feather), which in turn was derived from the Sanskrit *pet,* which means "to fly." At one time, the men employed as writing clerks were called "quill-drivers."

In an article published in *Antiques* (October 1940), H. Lyman Armes stated that "long after the Civil War, the grandfather of the man now pecking out his line on a typewriter was still putting fire and brimstone into his two Sunday sermons with a goose quill sharpened by himself." During the nineteenth century, classes were conducted to instruct students in the tedious art of cutting a quill nib. To sharpen the quill a knife was needed; hence the word "penknife" for the little instrument that was for so many years kept readily at hand in the inkstand drawer. However, as early as 1809 Joseph Braman had patented a machine for cutting a quill into separate nibs (points) to be slipped into the pen. This was the first use of a nib slipped into a holder. It proved most convenient and practical, and eventually it led to the steel nib. (The slit in any pen nib—goose quill, steel, or gold—controls the flow of ink to the paper.) Quill cutters are still seen in antique shops and shows, and they make interesting acquisitions for the collector of inkstands and wells. Some of the cutters available to collectors today were made in France.

It should also be mentioned that a tortoiseshell pen sometimes had a point made from a diamond or ruby, or from a small piece of thin sheet-gold lapped over the end of the tortoiseshell. In Chapter 17 of the Book of Jeremiah, there is a reference to a stylus tipped with a diamond.

The metal (bronze) pen has been known since the days of Pompeii, but metal pens were little used until the nineteenth century. In 1780 it is recorded that Samuel Harrison of Birmingham, England, made a steel pen for Dr. Joseph Priestley, and Colonial records at Williamsburg, Virginia, seem to indicate that steel pens were employed for a system of shorthand as early as 1786. In 1803, a tube or barrel-type pen, with edges that met to form a slit and the sides cut away as in the quill, was made in England by a man named Wise. In 1822 John Mitchell introduced machine-made pens. Steel slit pens, it is believed, were made first by James Perry (England, 1829); in a patent of 1830 Perry sought to make steel nibs more flexible by cutting one or more lateral slits on each side of the central slit. Joseph Gillot, another pen maker, elongated the points of nibs.

In the United States, Peregrine White, a Baltimore shoemaker and shot manufacturer, is credited with obtaining, on November 22, 1809, the first American pen patent for a "metallic writing pen." Steel pens were first produced commercially in 1858 by Richard Esterbrook, a manufacturer, at his factory in Camden, New Jersey. Steel pens were followed by pens of gold, silver, brass, and other metals, and in 1926 the first pens made of stainless steel appeared.

The fountain pen had been introduced earlier, but it did not become popular as a writing implement until it was produced in 1884 by L. E. Waterman. World War I gave impetus to its adoption—soldiers appreciated its convenience. Similarly, the invention of the ball-point pen dates back to the 1800s. A practical and workable version was perfected in 1937 by a Hungarian, Laszlo

141.   Pen and pencil boxes made of wood also appeal to collectors. The beautifully finished walnut one illustrated at the left has a brass plaque that reads "Mary E. Townsend, Jany 1st 1879." The black painted box has colorful Oriental figures on the hinged cover. The penholders shown here are pearl, ivory, and cut steel and have gold-filled nibs. The box of Esterbrook & Co. pen points—or nibs, as they were called—is interesting because it states: "The first steel pens manufactured in America were made by Richard Esterbrook in 1858."

Jozsef Biro, who lived in Argentina; but it was not widely used until World War II, when its long-lasting built-in supply of ink proved particularly convenient. The fiber pen was known to the Chinese in 1940. It was the Japanese, however, who made it successful in 1964.

Although all types of pens have their historical associations, it is the quill pen that is customarily linked with the historical period during which so many of today's world powers achieved their identity. Handcut colonial-style goose-quill pens are still made today.

The small, delicately wrought little penholders with gold nibs were doubtless gift items during the nineteenth and early twentieth centuries and deserve special attention from collectors. Some holders were of such material as mother-of-pearl and chased gold and had gold nibs; others were entirely chased silver or gold with matching gold or silver nibs. A number of these penholders are shown in Illustration No. 140. From the mint condition in which many of them are found, still reposing in the slim, narrow boxes they came in, it is evident that their owners considered them "too good to use." They are not only attractive items of historical significance to collect; when an inkstand has place for such a penholder, adding an appropriate one will increase its value.

Ink

Acquiring information about pens quite naturally leads one to the subject of ink. It is hardly a surprise to discover that the first liquids man used for writing were animal blood and the juices of plants. As we have already mentioned in the Introduction to this book, however, the history of ink is still much disputed because so little was recorded about it. Some historians claim that brown-colored sepia, the secretion from a small gland of the cuttlefish, antedated all other inks. Yet it seems to be more generally accepted that about 1200 B.C. (some say as early as 2697 B.C.) the Chinese perfected "India ink," also called "Indian ink," a mixture of soot produced by the smoke of pines and of lamp oil, combined with a gelatin made of donkey skin, musk being added to neutralize the odor.

According to some accounts, the Aztecs used an ink that was simply a watery solution of coloring matter. The Hebrews combined powdered charcoal and soot, sometimes adding gum to the mixture. For more than two hundred years they used this in inscribing their sacred scrolls. As explained in the Introduction, during the pre-Christian and early Christian eras, colored inks were made from dyes and pigments obtained from berries, plants, and animals, each color symbolizing a specific quality such as royalty, prosperity, vigor, sorrow, or love. Modern writing inks are dyes.

A powdered or block ink that had to be mixed fresh daily was in use during the Georgian period. It brought about the introduction of the quill cleaner, a container of some such material as silver or porcelain, which was sold separately or incorporated in an inkstand (see Chapter 5). Some quill cleaners had lead shot to expedite cleaning; at times, the quill pen might be plunged into the lead shot for storage when it was not in use. The later pen cleaner, also made of various materials, held a brush to clean the nib.

Mention should also be made of the numerous penwipers that were fashioned for gift-giving during the early years of the twentieth century. Felt was often used, cut into the shape of apples, strawberries, circles, squares, and the like. Sometimes five or six pieces of felt were held together with an embroidered "cover," or several layers of felt circles were pinked and fastened tightly together in the center with a button so that the layers curled upward to form a half-sphere. These were gay little gifts for schoolchildren, who also found them easy to make.

During the late eighteenth and nineteenth centuries, ink was usually made by a chemist and sold in labeled or embossed bottles of various sizes and shapes, either by him or at apothecary shops (they also made ink). It was even sold in some book shops. Much of the interest in collecting ink bottles lies in the fact that commercial ink bottles were so variously shaped: domed, rectangular, conical, square, and cylindrical, as well as figural—in the form of barrels, shoes, locomotives, and other objects. Small commercial ink bottles frequently served as inkwells for people who did not own more decorative ones, or who found the bottles more convenient to use. A friend recalls that during her childhood in Scotland her family regularly bought a small (about 1½ inches in diameter and about 2 inches high) bottle of ink for a penny, for household use.

Schools, offices, and other establishments where a supply of ink had to be kept on hand used master ink bottles not only of pottery in various sizes but also of glass. These bottles contained anywhere from a quarter of a pint to a gallon of ink, but the pint-sized bottle was the most popular.

To help prevent spilling when the ink was transferred from the master bottle to an individual well, there was a small "ink pourer." This resembled the contemporary Delft pitchers with elongated spouts much like a pelican's bill. The pourers we have seen average about three inches in diameter and four in height, and are made of copper or tin.

For the fastidious, during the late eighteenth and early nineteenth centuries, perfumed ink was sold in glass-stoppered bottles.

Those who had need of colored ink could choose red, green, or blue; generally colored ink was more expensive than black.

The ink on old documents is sometimes brown today because some of the inferior old inks faded when exposed to bright light or were subject to oxidation if they contained an iron component. Modern "iron gallotannate" inks are fortified with mineral acid to prevent oxidation as far as possible.

Large firms that produced ink finally forced the smaller companies out of business. The emergence of such large firms as Carter's Ink Company and Thaddeus Davids & Company also brought about another change: Before long, master ink bottles were made with built-in pouring devices that made ink pourers obsolete.

Pounce Pots and Sanders

The pounce pot, or sander, which through the centuries has been an important part of the inkstand, was also made during the eighteenth and nineteenth centuries as an individual item. Although pounce was discussed in an earlier chapter, for the reader's convenience we will go into some detail about it again.

The Oxford English Dictionary defines pounce as "a fine powder, such as pulverized sandarac or cuttle-shell, used to prevent ink from spreading in writing over an erasure or on unsized paper, and also to prepare the surface of parchment to receive writing." Hence, the writer who made a mistake when writing on unsized (unglazed) paper and laboriously scratched out his error with the necessary penknife obviously sprinkled pounce on the unglazed paper before he made his correction. According to old accounts, the pounce was rubbed in with the tooth of a dog or goat, but preferably with a burnished agate, to smooth the roughened surface of the paper and prepare it to receive the rewriting. Early parchment paper was oily, and to make it more receptive to ink, it too was powdered with pounce before use. The pounce was returned to the pot by pouring it through the piercings on the concave top surface of the container.

Pounce pots and sanders were of various shapes, conforming to the styles of inkstands in popular usage. They were made of the same variety of materials as the inkstands themselves—silver,

142. The two wooden sanders at left are approximately 3 inches in diameter and 3¼ inches in height. One is maple; the other, rosewood. The glass sander and glass well are approximately 1¾ inches square. Both have screw-type pewter caps. They are typical of the wells and sanders found in Victorian lap desks and small writing boxes.

pewter, brass, porcelain, pottery, and numerous others. During the early eighteenth century the plain round holes of the earlier metal pounce pots were given sawtooth edges; by mid-century the piercings had a curved shape, which made it easier to pour back the pounce after use.

With the advent of mechanically calendered paper in the latter part of the eighteenth century came a general demand for real sand, and a sander was included along with the vessel for pounce on some inkstands. It mut be mentioned, however, that the term "sander" was used often during the eighteenth century even before genuine sand came into popular use; the term appears frequently in old records, doubtless because to many people pounce *was* "sand."

During the nineteenth century, as commerce and travel increased, sanders were widely used both as individual items and as inclusions in lap desks and small traveling writing sets. In the United States, S. Silliman & Company made them to order in wood. Most of the separate sanders and pounce pots found today are either wood or metal, since few made of pottery and porcelain have survived. Some separate sanders of rosewood, maple, or other woods had an extended lip, a shallow cuplike formation around the top. This, of course, made pouring sand into and out of the receptacle a tidier process.

Sealing Wax, Seals, and Tapers

Before the advent of the machine-gummed envelope in the 1840s, sealing wax was used for important letters and documents. As described in Webster's *American Dictionary of the English Language* (1828), the sealing wax of that day was a "composition of gum-lacca and resin, colored with some pigment." In 1751, merchants in Williamsburg, Virginia, sold red and black sealing wax by the stick, the black being used when in mourning. Georgian tapersticks of expensive English beeswax, also called "tea-candlesticks," were used to melt the sealing wax. These tapers were so sweet-smelling that, from about 1740 to 1770, they were burned in their inkstand holders as much for their desirable odor as for the practical purpose of melting sealing wax.

Those who wished to personalize their sealing wax could impress a design into the warm wax by means of an ornately executed little "stamp" (seal) bearing the design in intaglio—a monogram, the head of a knight, the figure of an animal, or some other decorative device. Such small stamping implements were made of gold, silver, quartz, and various other materials or combinations. Many people collect them today, and they are seen quite often at antique shows.

During the period when sealing wax was popularly used, wafers of paste were customarily used to seal unimportant letters and papers. The thin, brittle wafer is described in *The Oxford English Dictionary* as "a small disk of flour mixed with gum and non-poisonous colouring matter, or a gelatine or the like similarly coloured, which when moistened is used for sealing letters, attaching papers, or receiving the impression of a seal." Colonial Williamsburg, Virginia, records refer to them as being of various sizes, including "large"; in Therle Hughes's book *Small Decorative Antiques*, the wafer is mentioned as being the size of a shilling. Wafers were made in "wafer irons" placed over a charcoal fire, and were cut into disks with steel punches. Red and black wafers were sold at the Williamsburg printing office in 1750; "Wafers," "Dutch Sealing Wafers," and "Vermillion Wafers" were advertised for sale by early Williamsburg merchants. Black wafers, like black sealing wax, were for mourning use, as was mourning paper, another item sold by the early Williamsburg merchants. When wafers were outdated, and after stamps had come into use, the small wafer box that was a component of some inkstands or sold as a separate article was used for stamps.

Paste, Mucilage, and Glue Pots and Bottles

Pots for mucilage, paste, or glue make good companions for a collection of inkstands, wells, and bottles. Many made of pressed or cut glass are as attractive as the small nineteenth-century scent bottles. These pretty little pots were made in the latter part of the nineteenth century and into the twentieth century. Most are of clear glass, although they probably were made in colored glass too. Usually such a pot had a sterling or silver-plated screw-on cap with a hole in it through which a silver-handled brush was thrust into the glue, paste, or mucilage. In fact, the pots are distant cousins to the clear or aqua glass bottles with labels or embossings in which these substances were commercially sold. (Most makers of ink also produced adhesives—Carter's Ink Company, Sanford Manufacturing Company, and others.) The bottles, whatever their shape, averaged about two inches across and approximately two to three inches high, most being conical (either plain or fluted). Larger bottles were made for the adhesives needed in offices, schools, and such establishments.

Incidentally, glue is made from fish and the bones, hoofs, skin, and other waste parts of animals; mucilage is prepared from gelatinous substances found in plants.

143. Presented here are two pressed glass paste pots, with separate sterling silver lids and sterling handled brushes, and an all-sterling paste pot with brush. The three sterling letter-openers with mother-of-pearl blades are other collectible items related to the ritual of writing.

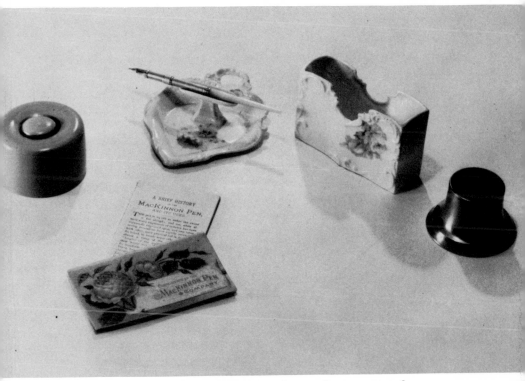

144. Both porcelain and metal penholders and pen cleaners are collectible desk accessories. The porcelain pieces here are hand-painted with floral designs. The pen cleaner at left, more than 2½ inches in diameter, is rose-colored porcelain with a gold band around the separate cover. A brush is affixed to the side of the interior of the vessel to clean the pen nib.

Other Writing Accouterments

In the late Victorian period, more and more writing accessories of porcelain, silver, and various other materials were made, until it would seem that only the largest desktop could accommodate all of them. During the early years of the twentieth century, when desk "sets" were commonly used, there seemed to be more such appointments than a desk surface could hold and still leave space to write.

Some of the porcelain writing accessories were daintly painted, probably with the Victorian female in mind. These included pen

racks, letter racks, and stamp boxes. Pen racks of silver were also sold; even silver-handled magnifying glasses were made. (Recently, collectors have begun to take the mother-of-pearl, silver, or gold handles from old canes and affix them to magnifying glasses. Though not entirely old, these "married" creations look handsome in company with old inkstands and inkwells.)

At the turn of the century the desire to own a desk "set" with its accompanying inkstand was heightened by the appearance of the Tiffany "status" pieces. But office desks too became crowded with a miscellany of such appurtenances designed to lighten the burden of letter writing and account keeping. There were metal or glass paperweights, rocker blotters of silver and other metals and porcelain, fancy embossed-metal letter clips, and calendars, holders for pens, memorandum pads, and letter scales. Today, all sorts of paperweights—even commercial business weights—and many of the desk-set type of writing accessories are exciting collector interest.

145.   Shown here are a magnifying glass with a handle of sterling silver and mother-of-pearl (formerly an umbrella handle), a sterling pen rack, a Scandinavian silver sander, a crystal and silver box, and sterling silver pens, all of which make attractive ornaments on a desk to complement inkstands and inkwells.

◀

146.   Transfer-decorated wooden desk accessories are among the "new antiques" now being sought. The items shown here are Scottish and English, although many American pieces are to be found. The memo pad and the letter opener bear scenes of the Robert Burns Monument and are marked "Made from wood which grew on the banks of the Doon." The pen and pencil box has scenes of Dryburgh and Melrose abbeys. The wood was grown on the lands of Abbotsford. The small box depicts Windsor Castle; the pen is a Robinson. The cast-metal spindle-file has an embossed base similar to the metal paperweights used a half century and more ago.

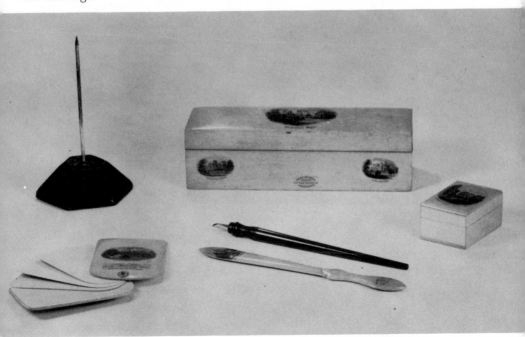

Writing Accessories in Pictures

Many artists who painted famous statesmen or historic events included quill pens, inkstands, or inkwells either in the background or as essential features of the scene. To name a few paintings of this kind: Hogarth's "Marriage a la Mode—The Contract" (1743–45) shows a marriage contract being signed at a table holding an inkstand with a candle, inkpot, bell, and probably a sandbox. Eighteenth-century American artist John Greenwood made impor-

tant use of a quill pen in his portrait of Dr. M. Elgers—he showed the doctor writing with one. In 1789, Charles Willson Peale portrayed Benjamin Franklin sitting at a table with his lightning rods and a manuscript placed beside an oval silver inkstand with two vessels; a quill pen reposes in the quill rest of one of these vessels.

Prints have been made of many such paintings, and today collectors of inkstands, wells, and bottles find these reproductions of particular interest. They accent the historical significance of a collection. Framed in old curly maple, one or two such prints make an appropriate wall decoration near a display of wells or stands.

147. General O. H. La Granbe, superintendent of the United States Mint at San Francisco, is shown at his desk there in 1874, using a Victorian inkstand. The mint survived the ravages of the San Francisco earthquake in 1905.

Bibliography

Altman, Violet and Seymour. *The Book of Buffalo Pottery.* New York: Crown Publishers, Inc., 1969.

Amaya, Mario. *Tiffany Glass.* New York: Walker and Company, 1968.

Bacci, Mina. *European Porcelain.* London: Paul Hamlyn, 1962.

Barber, Edwin Atlee. *The Pottery and Porcelain of the United States,* 3rd ed. New York: G. P. Putnam's Sons, 1909.

Barret, Richard Carter. *Bennington Pottery and Porcelain.* New York: Bonanza Books, 1958.

Bedford, John. *All Kinds of Small Boxes.* New York: Walker and Company, 1965.

————. *Paperweights.* New York: Walker and Company, 1968.

————. *Staffordshire Pottery Figures*. New York: Walker and Company, 1965.

Bergstrom, Evangeline. *Old Glass Paperweights*. New York: Crown Publishers, Inc., 1947.

Bly, John. *Discovering Hallmarks on English Silver*. Herts, England: Shire Publications, 1969.

Butler, Joseph T. *American Antiques 1800–1900*. New York: The Odyssey Press, 1965.

Cole, Ann Kilborn. *How to Collect the "New" Antiques*. New York: David McKay Co., Inc., 1966.

Covill, William E., Jr. *Ink Bottles and Inkwells*. Taunton, Mass.: William S. Sullwold, 1971.

Daniel, Dorothy. *Cut and Engraved Glass*. New York: M. Barrows & Co., 1950.

DeVoe, Shirley Spaulding. *English Papier-Mâché of the Georgian and Victorian Periods*. Middletown, Conn.: Wesleyan University Press, 1968.

Drepperd, Carl W. *ABC's of Old Glass*. New York: Award Books, 1968.

————. *Victorian, the Cinderella of Antiques*. New York: Award Books, 1970.

Durdik, Jan; Dagmar Hejdová; Dagmar Hniková; Ludmila Kybalová; Miroslav Mudra; Dagmar Stará and Libuse Uresolva. *The Pictorial Encyclopedia of Antiques*. London, New York, Sydney, Toronto: The Hamlyn Publishing Group Ltd., 1970.

Earle, Alice Morse. *China Collecting in America*. New York: Charles Scribner's Sons, 1892.

Edwards, Ralph, and Ramsey, L. G. G. (eds.). *The Connoisseur's Complete Period Guides to English Antiques*. New York: Bonanza, 1968.

Frantz, Henri. *French Pottery and Porcelain*. New York: Charles Scribner's Sons, n.d.

Godden, Geoffrey, A. *An Illustrated Encyclopedia of British Pottery and Porcelain.* New York: Bonanza, 1966.

Gordon, Hampden. *The Lure of Antiques.* London: John Murray, 1964.

Gorley, Jean. *Wedgwood.* New York: M. Barrows & Co., Inc., 1950.

Honey, William B. *Old English Porcelain.* New York: Whittlesey House, 1948.

Hughes, G. Bernard. *The Collector's Pocket Book of China.* New York: Award Books, 1970.

Hughes, Therle. *Small Decorative Antiques.* London: Lutterworth Press, 1959.

Kerfoot, John B. *American Pewter.* New York: Crown Publishers, Inc., 1942.

Koch, Robert. *Louis C. Tiffany's Glass–Bronzes–Lamps.* New York: Crown Publishers, Inc., 1971.

Laughlin, Ledlie I. *Pewter in America.* 2 vols. Boston: Houghton Mifflin Company, 1940.

Lee, Ruth Webb. *Nineteenth-Century Art Glass.* New York: M. Barrows & Co., 1952.

———. *Sandwich Glass.* Framingham Center, Mass.: Published by Author, 1939.

———. *Victorian Glass.* Northboro Mass.: Published by Author, 1944.

McClinton, Katharine Morrison. *Antique Collecting for Everyone.* New York: Bonanza, n.d.

———. *Collecting American Antiques.* New York: Gramercy, Publishing Co., 1950.

———. *Handbook of Popular Antiques.* New York: Bonanza, 1945.

McKearin, Helen and George S. *American Glass.* New York: Crown Publishers, Inc., 1941.

———. *Two Hundred Years of American Blown Glass.* New York: Crown Publishers, Inc., 1962.

Mankowitz, Wolf. *Wedgwood*. London: B. T. Botsford, Ltd., 1953.

Montagu, Jennifer. *Bronzes–Pleasures and Treasures*. New York: G. P. Putnam's Sons, 1963.

Penkala, Maria. *European Pottery*. Rutland, Vt.: Charles E. Tuttle Company, 1968.

Peter, Mary. *Collecting Victoriana*. New York: Frederick A. Praeger, 1968.

Revi, Albert Christian. *Nineteenth Century Glass: Its Genesis and Development*. New York: Thomas Nelson & Sons, 1959.

Savage, George. *Eighteenth Century English Porcelain*. London: Spring Books, 1964.

Spargo, John. *Early American Pottery and China*. New York: The Century Co., 1926.

Thorn, C. Jordan. *Handbook of Old Pottery and Porcelain Marks*. New York: Tudor Publishing Co., 1947.

Trimble, Alberta C. *Modern Porcelain*. New York: Harper and Brothers, 1962.

Van Tassel, Valentine. *American Glass*. New York: Gramercy Publishing Company, 1950.

Watkins, Lura Woodside. *American Glass and Glassmaking*. New York: Chanticleer Press, 1950.

————. *Cambridge Glass 1818–1888*. Boston: Marshall Jones Co., 1930.

Wenham, Edward. *Domestic Silver of Great Britain*. London: Oxford University Press, 1931.

Wills, Geoffrey. *Practical Guide to Antique Collecting*. New York: Arc Books, 1961.

Winchester, Alice. *How to Know American Antiques*. New York: New American Library of World Literature, Inc., 1935.

Wyler, Seymour B. *The Book of Old Silver*. New York: Crown Publishers, Inc., 1937.

————. *The Book of Sheffield Plate.* New York: Crown Publishers, Inc., 1949.

Miscellaneous

Glass Center, Corning, New York. Corning Glass Center, Corning, New York, 1958.

Glass from the Corning Museum of Glass. Corning Glass Center, Corning, New York, 1965.

Goodwin, Mary R. *Eighteenth Century Writing Equipment.* Colonial Williamsburg Research Department, 1964.

"Inkstands and Inkwells." *The Antique Trader,* 30 May 1972.

McClinton, Katharine Morrison. "Art Silver." *The Antique Trader,* 3 October 1972.

Printed data concerning Gorham inkwells. The Gorham Company.

Printed data regarding writing pens and the history of ink. Parker Pen Company, n.d.

Wehreven, Austin C. "Art Deco." *Christian Science Monitor,* 23 August 1971.

Wenham, Edward. "Standishes and Inkstands." *International Studio,* November 1927.

Winters, Henry. *An Appreciation of Tiffany Favrile Glass.* Published by Author, n.d.

Index

Page numbers in italics refer to illustrations.